Creating and Dominating New Markets

Creating and Dominating New Markets

PETER MEYER

AMACOM

American Management Association

New York • Atlanta • Brussels • Buenos Aires • Chicago • London • Mexico City
San Francisco • Shanghai • Tokyo • Toronto • Washington, D.C.

This publication is designed to provide accurate and authoritative information in regard to the subject matter covered. It is sold with the understanding that the publisher is not engaged in rendering legal, accounting, or other professional service. If legal advice or other expert assistance is required, the services of a competent professional person should be sought.

Library of Congress Cataloging-in-Publication Data

Meyer, Peter, 1954–
    Creating and dominating new markets / Peter Meyer.
       p. cm.
    Includes bibliographical references and index.
    ISBN 0-8144-0678-5
    1. New products. 2. Marketing. 3. Creative ability in business. I. Title.

    HF5415.153 .M493   2002
    658.8—dc21

2001053663

Printing number

10 9 8 7 6 5 4 3 2 1

Contents

Acknowledgments   vii

Introduction   ix

PART 1: Strategies for Creating and Dominating New Markets   **1**

CHAPTER 1: The Mystique and Challenges of New Markets   3

CHAPTER 2: Balancing Your Resources and Your Opportunities   29

CHAPTER 3: It's the Problem That Matters   51

CHAPTER 4: Choosing the Best Risk   71

CHAPTER 5: What New Markets Are Available to You?   93

PART 2: Applications of the Strategies   **111**

CHAPTER 6: Funding the New Market Effort   113

CHAPTER 7: What Role Does the Customer Play? 141

CHAPTER 8: Building and Dominating Markets
Through Involvement 159

CHAPTER 9: What Is the Role of Information
Technology? 181

CHAPTER 10: Using Credibility in Creating and
Dominating Markets 201

CHAPTER 11: What's Next? 217

Notes 227

Index 233

Acknowledgments

Dozens of people make a book into a good book. Some encourage the right ideas, some help target them. Some just sponsor them. In this case, numerous corporate executives in the United States, Europe, and Asia played critical roles in lending ideas, comments, and suggestions. A number of executives, some direct competitors with each other, have graciously worked with us to provide examples. For the ones who were willing to put competitive issues aside, I offer a special thank you. It is not always easy to decide that you wish to open your business up, and I greatly appreciate the fact you have done that here.

Likewise, several people took an incredible amount of time to look over the work and help improve it. If you find this work valuable, you should say a silent thank you to David Ludwig, Lori Trippel, Adrienne Hickey, and especially Ilse Meyer. These four have made this a much better work. I have nothing but profound thanks for their help.

Inspiration comes from many people. For me, Bruce Smith has been a wonderful source.

Several magazines have been gracious enough to let me reprint popular articles that they have run. I owe special thanks to Jan Collins of *Business & Economic Review*, Dennis Organ of *Busi-*

ness Horizons, and Fred Knight of *Business Communications Review.*

If you don't like the work, none of these people deserves the blame. The blame rests with me. If you find errors, please tell me so that I can fix them for the next readers. Drop me a line at Peter@MeyerGrp.com. If you find that you want more information and examples, we will be creating an index of successes. Send me a note and I'll let you know how to get access.

Most important of all, there is one person who made this all possible: Eva Meyer. Not just this book, but the world itself is infinitely better because she is here.

Introduction

Ever since we had markets, businesspeople have wanted to find new ones and then find ways to corner them. Being Daimler at the turn of the century or America Online at the beginning of the Internet age is a wonderful goal—but a hard one to make real without planning. This book is about what it takes to plan and then create and dominate new markets.

The Allure of New Markets

But why bother? Why are new markets a Holy Grail for business owners and managers? If you can create a new market and then be the dominant player, all kinds of benefits start to accrue to you. For example:

▶ You can take the time to do things right the first time you do them. Less calendar pressure allows for more creativity, which can make your work more fun.

▶ You can make and survive mistakes. Since you have no competition, operational excellence is not as important as it is when you are in existing markets.

▶As the only supplier, you can work with the customers to define the market so that it helps both of you.

▶You can recruit people faster and more easily as a market-leading company. With no competition, you are automatically the largest and most important player.

▶Your stock may be worth much more if you show an ability to create and dominate new markets. Wall Street often rewards entries into new markets.

▶You have independence. When you enter a new market, you are alone. Many people prefer to be market visionaries.

▶You can price to market instead of to competitive pressure. You have a chance at faster and greater profitability.

The attraction of new markets isn't difficult to understand: You can make a lot of money, have a lot more fun, and get better people to work with you. Who wouldn't want that?

What Happens in New Markets?

You can find many examples of companies that have created markets and then dominated them. I'll define new markets in detail in Chapter 1, but consider the reputations of Nike (athletic shoes as urban uniform), Amazon.com (book sales via the Internet), and Apple Computer (desktop publishing). These are businesses that found a way to create a market when none had existed before. What is more important, they found a way to keep it going and to sustain their business.

What makes up this pattern of success? It starts with the idea for a market that did not exist before, and then goes out to test it. Sometimes one person has the idea and brings product to reality. Steve Jobs was sure that the world was ready for desktop publishing. However, just as often others find the idea. Celgene Corp. did not create the market for Thalomid (thalidomide) among HIV patients. They found it when doctors and patients started to use the drug for HIV disease without Food and Drug Administration (FDA) approval.

New market successes often seem accidental. They do not have to be. Failures to create new markets are legion. Your attempt does not have to be one of those. You can follow systematic strategies for success. This book is about those strategies.

Whom Is This Book Written For?

I wrote this book for owners and managers who want to emulate market builders yet reduce their risk as they do so. It is not academic in style, although it does build from research and casework. The book presents the principles and strategies that have worked and then some applications as examples. Perhaps most important, the next chapters suggest a different way to look at your business. By examining your company or division through a new lens, you have the opportunity to see things that you may otherwise have missed.

Why Do You Care?

Most businesses are in competitive markets. There is little room for error, margins are under duress from price attacks by other vendors, and the chances for market expansion are limited. Creating a new midpriced female doll with a "personality" puts your company in direct competition with Mattel, a competition that will be hard to win.

Worse, existing markets are repetitive and boring. One reason your best people may be leaving is to find new and interesting projects to work on. Making a better cell phone is exciting, but not forever. Remember Steve Jobs's comment to lure John Sculley away from PepsiCo to become president of Apple? "Do you want to make sugar water for the rest of your life?" New markets can be intensely interesting and satisfying as well as profitable.

What Should You Take Away from This Book?

Plan on getting two things from this book. First, plan on gaining a different understanding of how to create and dominate new markets. Markets are not found; someone creates them. You can be that someone if you choose. New markets are not easy, but they are very rewarding.

Second, plan on getting specific applications and ideas from this book. Some will be directly from my suggestions and drawn from the experience of others. Some of the best ideas will be the result of suggestions that you adapt to fit your own environment.

When you are done, you will look at new markets in a different way. You will have the tools to go out and take action in new arenas. The important thing is to take the action systematically and successfully. With the material that you are about to read, you can combine those two qualities. Then you can reap the rewards of creating and dominating new markets.

Creating and Dominating New Markets

Strategies for Creating and Dominating New Markets

1

The Mystique and Challenges of New Markets

As you look to grow your business, you may be asking:

▶Why create new markets?

▶Are there hurdles to overcome?

▶Do I create new markets, or do I find them?

▶Are there some common denominators to success?

▶How can I repeatedly create and dominate new markets?

This chapter is a start down the path to creating and dominating new markets. You will find short answers to these questions and a tour of the basics. Once you understand these principles, the entire process of creating and dominating markets gets much more systematic, predictable, and repeatable. Once you have repeatable success, you can fine-tune your work.

This book continues in two parts. The chapters in Part 1 will help you identify strategies for creating and dominating new markets. An Applications section of the book provides further details and tactics for those strategies, giving you the examples from which to build.

Although you'll find many successes detailed in the book, your own business is unique, and each business will approach new markets in a different way. The dozens of examples that are in this book should help you to design the right mix of strategies and applications for your own enterprise. As the chief executive or general manager of your business, the final design is up to you, but the first question has to be: Why create new markets?

Why Go After New Markets?

Why are new markets so desirable? Because they are exciting, profitable, and forgiving.

The Excitement of New Markets

The excitement of creating and dominating a market is very real. Some of that exhilaration comes from the sheer joy of creating something that did not exist before you stepped in. Many senior managers have the urge to produce something new. Doing something no one else has done, going where no one has gone before—these are very attractive ideas for managers who spend most of their days dealing with familiar issues and solving other people's problems. For many, creating tomorrow's new markets is simply more fun than solving today's problems. Fun can be an important part of getting repeatable success.

The Profit in New Markets

New markets can be more profitable than existing ones. In competitive markets you always face the pressure to reduce prices to match competitors. Someone always seems to be willing to "buy business" by selling at very low margins. When you have no competition, you can price to the customer's sense of value, not another vendor's sense of desperation. If the customer is willing to pay more, you can get that additional income. Your margins increase, and you can get a consistent flow of cash to add to the bank account and use to fund future growth.

Another reason to create a market is that the equities exchanges may reward you for your efforts. The perception of value is not always rational, and managing stock prices is a difficult task. However, if you announce that your business is creating a new market and get analyst support, your stock price may rise consistently. You run the risk of losing any gain if the new markets fail, but a company that consistently succeeds (and succeeding half the time is consistent) makes for an appealing story on the stock exchanges.

The Forgiving Nature of New Markets

Dominance in markets can make existing, competitive markets more forgiving as well. If you are in an expensive price or feature war in a tough market today, perhaps it would be great to have other resources to subsidize the battle. If so, a captive market with high margins and good cash flow could be that source of time, people, and money.

Consider the history of Microsoft Corp.'s online network. Through its Microsoft Network (MSN), the company wanted to enter and dominate the Internet service provider (ISP) market. Microsoft's existing competition? Well-designed offerings from America Online (AOL), Yahoo!, and others. Microsoft's management team knew that they would have to invest considerable time, human resources, and money to be competitive. Thanks to Microsoft's dominance of the operating systems market in the 1990s, the company had the resources to cover the cost of making multiple challenges to AOL.

If you are the only player in a market, you can make mistakes and not lose share to your rivals—you don't have any rivals. You can price to market and take advantage of the lack of competition to increase your margins.

That tolerance for mistakes also creates a great training ground for executives. You may have people who would benefit from the experience and maturation of taking an idea to success. Since your core business should not be an experiment, it may make sense to ask your managers to go build a new market. With good design, the worst case is that you will lose some money and find that they are not good managers. The best case is that the new market will pan out for you and subsidize the training of your next great senior executive.

The forgiving nature of new markets opens the potential to make your own rules. Existing markets have structures that all participants respect. If you offer luxury goods, you don't sell through down-market chain stores because your normal channels will rebel if you do. Creating a new market allows you to distance your business from the restrictions of history and write your own rules.

Potential Benefits You Accrue in New Markets

▶You can realize high margins.

▶You can subsidize or protect other market efforts.

▶You can gain from appreciation of your stock's value.

▶You can experiment and fail, but still survive.

▶You can groom new executives.

You can keep the company from stagnating as old markets stabilize. Sometimes companies break the rules to create new markets (see Figure 1-1). In a major break with traditional busi-

Figure 1-1. Breaking rules to create new markets.

Product	Rule-Breaking Approach
Navigator	Gave unknown product to unknown customer set to create the market Delivered unfinished products to users as part of the testing cycle
ICQ (chat software)	Gave its product away to create the market with no revenue plan
Land Camera	Asked users to participate in the film development process by printing their own pictures
Thalomid	Seized upon opportunity when doctors experimentally administered thalidomide to HIV patients, creating a new market in anti-HIV drugs

ness models, Mirabilis Ltd. (now a property of AOL) created a software product and gave it away free. The old rule was that you gave products away only to lead to further revenue from other product sales. Cellular service providers give phones away in the United States, but tie each "gift" to a lucrative services contract. You might give razors away, but you have razor blades to sell immediately. Mirabilis followed a different path. The company had no revenue, and no plans for any. Yet, in 1998, America Online paid more than a quarter billion dollars for Mirabilis. The product, as part of AOL Instant Messenger, still dominates the market.

The problem is that it is far from easy to create and dominate a market. For every Amazon.com, there are several companies like Pointcast and Webvan that have burned up hundreds of millions of dollars trying and failing to create a viable market.

What Are New Markets?

A new market is new to everyone. Just because a market may be new to you does not make it a new market. Consider the market for human immunodeficiency virus (HIV) treatments. Burroughs Wellcome took a drug for breast cancer and found that it would slow the replication of the HIV virus. This antiviral medicine, AZT, was the first major breakthrough for treatment of the disease. Burroughs Wellcome created a new market with the compound, and AZT still plays a dominant and profitable role in that market today. (Burroughs Wellcome no longer exists as an independent company. AZT is now manufactured and sold by GlaxoSmithKline.)

Today several companies market disposable cameras for the consumer market. The cameras are inexpensive, easy to use, and produce good pictures. They sell well to families and tourists. However, the companies that introduced disposable cameras did not create that consumer market. Edwin Land did in 1949. By inventing and producing a camera that would print a picture while the consumer waited, he took a hobbyist product into a new consumer market. By using innovative technologies and jealously guarding his patents, Land built his company, Polaroid Corp., into a major U.S. corporation in the 1950s and continued to dominate that market for years.

The Polaroid Land Camera was a new device. What about selling an existing product to a population that was previously unavailable? When the analog cell phone market in the United States seemed to become saturated, manufacturers modified the same core products to be salable in the People's Republic of China. A new market came to be because a new population became available as consumers.

Some products are line extensions, not market creators. Today, many companies make consumer cameras that are far easier to use than cameras were a few years ago. Manufacturers improve Internet servers, incrementally, on an almost weekly basis. My local grocery has six kinds of Tide detergent on the shelf. None of these enhanced products are market creators. For the purposes of this book, disposable cameras, better servers, and Tide with Bleach are line extensions. They helped change their markets and brought considerable revenues to their manufacturers, but they did not help create a new market where none existed before. The cell phone markets in the People's Republic of China, sales to HIV patients, and consumer photography were new markets. In Chapter 5, you will find a model to classify new markets. You'll also find more information on how to increase your chances of success when you build them.

Where Are New Markets?

By definition, new markets are nowhere—yet. Like any idea that is not yet elaborated, they exist in potential. The best way to identify the location of a new market is to look for the location of a problem. Let's return to pharmaceuticals as a quick example. (Chapter 3 examines this issue of problem identification in detail.)

In the 1970s, HIV disease was still rare. As the next decade rolled out, the disease expanded to become a major personal, social, and political problem. HIV patients were a market in potential but not yet organized into a viable form.

AZT helped change that potential into a new market. The problem defined the market, not the solution. Which company provided the solution was unimportant to the customers. Burroughs Wellcome was the company with AZT, but it might just as well have been Schering-Plough or Bristol-Myers Squibb with different drugs. A market is not the product that the supplier creates. A market starts with the need that the product can satisfy. When you combine need and product, you can start to create a new market. Where video-on-demand to the home has failed as a product, AOL, HIV treatments, and the Polaroid Land

Camera succeeded because customers perceived the needs intensely for these products.

Four Common Denominators of Success in New Markets

▶When you look at the companies that have been successful at creating new markets, you can see several common key elements. You will increase your chance of repeated and systematic success by following these principles.

1. *Customer-driven markets work better than vendor-driven markets.* Many new markets come from ideas driven by a sole visionary. Steve Jobs and Steve Wozniak created the Apple Computer with little market analysis. Henry Ford designed his first cars without a great deal of marketing and customer input. Netscape Communications created its Navigator browser without relying on a marketing study. These are impressive successes, but they are outweighed by the vast number of products that failed, even though someone had a great vision.

Recent examples show the difference between internally driven ideas and customer-driven markets. As interesting as an online grocery delivery service might have been, it did not create a market. As much fun as "push" Internet technology might have been to design and bring to market, consumers were not excited enough to keep it going. Home automation still has not taken off. Even after a decade, Integrated Services Digital Network (ISDN) voice and data service may still be a solution in search of a problem in the United States.

To reduce the risk you run when you create new markets, locate markets that have real potential. Don't measure potential by the possible number of users, but by the severity of the problem as a specific number of users perceive it. When Glaxo Wellcome (now merged and part of GlaxoSmithKline) looked at the potential for the company's new migraine remedy, Imitrex, it did not look at the painkiller market. Why? Headache sufferers did not define Imitrex's potential. Most patients do not need Imitrex to resolve the pain. The exception—migraine patients. Severity of the need, as customers perceive it, is what drives the potential volume in your new market. (For more on how to identify the right problems to create markets, see Chapter 3.)

2. *Follow one of two lower-risk paths.* Netscape created and dominated a new market the riskiest way when the company's founders chose to develop a new product for a new market. Edwin Land broke through at a lower risk, developing a new product (instant photography) for a known market. Motorola reduced its risk by taking a known product (analog cell phones) into unknown markets (developing countries.) All three strategies worked, but Polaroid and Motorola took a lower-risk path. Since the risk of failure is high, it makes sense to reduce the risk when you can. (For more on the two lowest-risk paths, please see Chapter 5.)

3. *Be willing to ignore opportunities.* Many managers look for opportunities, and then jump to take advantage of the ones that they can reach. As counterintuitive as it may seem, jumping to opportunities as they arise can make it difficult to create and dominate new markets. If your market concept was sound last week, it should still be sound this week. Diluting efforts will make it harder for any effort to succeed. To win at new markets, stay on one track. (For more examples of this principle, see Chapter 2.)

4. *Start with cross-functional teams and leadership.* One common denominator of success in new markets is that a leader who crosses organizational boundaries manages the effort. No single function can do this work for you. Marketing is not well suited for the task, nor is engineering or finance. You want your sales team to focus on this quarter's revenue, but you'll need their input on the new market. The role of the business leader is to span vertical functions as the business focuses on new markets. This role is critical to creating and dominating new markets.

What Is the Role of the Business Leader?

As the leader of a business unit, you have a specific role to play in making a new market work by ensuring that cross-functional teams keep the correct focus. To succeed, you must test every idea and tear it apart—and ask the correct questions. As the guide to the effort of creating a new market, you have to ensure that your managers look where most functional managers are unwilling and untrained to look. Then you have to guide your team to ask the right questions. The work is important and difficult.

Success requires high-quality work from each of your engineering, manufacturing, marketing, sales, and financial teams. The output of that work will put you into a highly competitive market that will reward your ability to choose the right channel and to offer a little more value at a lower cost.

You can use four different paths to create a new market (as shown in Figure 1-2), balancing the products that you know well with customer sets with which you are familiar. (Chapter 5 gives recommendations and examples of each strategy.) However, this balance of product and market is a task that a general executive should manage. You cannot rely on marketing, sales, or finance

Figure 1-2. Paths to new markets.

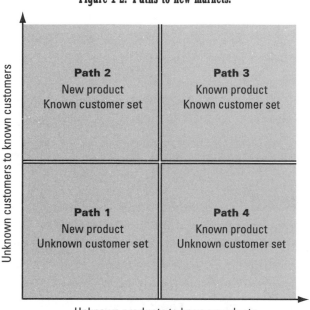

Unknown products to known products

to take the lead role. Entering new markets requires someone to bridge those roles.

The Marketing Team

Your marketing team can help to define what will sell to existing customers and how the product should look to a defined market. The problem comes in uncovering new markets; here, marketing is less helpful. Marketing and product groups are often too close to their own disciplines to be able to suggest the correct solution.

Customers often have no idea that they make up a new market. The first fax machines were priced at about $1,000 each and were marketed to work with a limited set of customers. Participants in the market that eventually evolved (i.e., small businesses, departments, and home offices) told marketers that they did not see a need for the product and wouldn't spend the money to buy fax machines. Marketing teams from the early fax companies listened and focused the product and the pitch on the high end. Relying purely on customer input would have missed the fax market entirely. Marketing has a role to play in new market development, but it is not the traditional function. For an example of a better way to use the skill set of your marketing team, see Chapter 7.

The Sales Team

Your sales team is another important resource that cannot usually lead the effort. To compete successfully in known markets, you must dedicate your best salespeople to your current products and extensions to those products. Diverting these specialists into other areas, even for a short while, puts your existing revenue stream at risk. Nonetheless, your salespeople and channels still play a role in creating new markets.

The value of your sales team or channel is in *accidentally* exploring new markets for you. Occasionally, you'll find someone who goes outside the rules and finds a new customer set. For example, a set of doctors may take your pharmaceuticals off-label (i.e., use them for unapproved treatments) and in the process uncover a potential new market. Celgene tapped into a new market just this way with Thalidomide. Your sales team knows when this activity happens. Use that knowledge to find out how and why customers are going outside normal boundaries. These are serendipities that you can watch for and use to your advantage.

Serendipity, like mutation, succeeds infrequently. However, one discovery may become a billion-dollar product like AZT.

Make sure you know when someone starts using your products in a way that you did not intend.

The Finance Team

Financial modeling is an attractive tool, but it's usually misleading in creating and dominating new markets. The skills that members of your financial team use on existing markets are less useful here. When you decide to extend an existing product line, you can immediately apply numerous financial report cards. You can systematically choose the volume, margins, and price elasticity with a spreadsheet. The answer is predictable.

Creating a new market does not lend itself to such accuracy. You can't know the volumes or attractive price points. Your costs are just as unknown. Even if you know what it would cost to make your product (and you probably do not), how can you know what it will really cost to attract the buyers?

Good financial analysis has one primary use in market creation—it may show you the break points you must reach to become operational and profitable, or when to leave the new market. The rest is up to your own judgment.

Betting the Business

In the end, the analysis will float to the manager or team that can feel comfortable making the call. From that vantage you are in a better position to see the paths to unthought-of markets and to markets in new geographies. However, you can't decide to create and dominate a new market with numbers, market data, or sales data. As uncomfortable as it may be, the real data will never be there.

You will be betting the future on a problem, the one you

hope to solve. Your decision will come down to how you answer these two questions:

► Are you solving a problem that will resonate with people?

► Do you have a solution in search of a problem?

The new market becomes a gut call. That is the province of a top executive or owner. You have to ask the right questions, determine if you can get market acceptance, and then make that call.

As you look at the opportunity and risk from new markets, here are some key questions to ask of users, your team, and yourself:

Questions to Ask to Build a New Market

To the users:

► If you could do this new function, would you get really excited? What would get you really excited?

► What problems tend to repeat at the top of your action list?

To your team and yourself:

► Are we solving a real problem? Or do we have a solution in search of a problem?

► What are the unexpected common denominators among our end-users? Do these common denominators suggest more than a product line extension?

► Are we watching our sales team in case it finds unexpected markets?

▶What do we have to do to be first to market acceptance?

▶What are our customers doing in today's market that we never expected? Can we see a new market from that?

▶Where are the break points to hit before we can (1) enter a market and (2) make a return? What is the point to leave?

▶Is the inherent value there for the end-buyer or for a third party?

▶Can we identify a channel that will get that value to the buyer very quickly and efficiently?

▶Can we establish a good relationship directly with the buyers, no matter which channel we use?

To yourself:

▶Does my instinct support my analytical decision to try to create the market?

Six Hurdles to Clear

After the common denominators to success, consider these hurdles. All can be cleared if you take the time to prepare before you reach them. You can speed past each hurdle, but not by chance.

Hurdle 1: Funding the Work Internally with Time, People, and Money

New markets can cost you a substantial amount of time, people, and money. When you invest a year and your best people in a new market, they may be great investments, but they are unavailable for other projects. If you enter a market that works, this is fine. If you enter a market that fails, you may miss other markets that would do very well. You don't have infinite resources; new markets can suck them up and reduce your ability to reach other opportunities (see Chapter 2 for an example).

Hurdle 2: Finding Key External Support

Your own investments are not the only concern. You may find it difficult to locate supporters and keep the resources flowing if your attention appears to be wavering into unknown markets.

In some business sectors, investors are willing to commit resources into new markets. In the year 2000, Internet business-to-business ventures, pharmaceuticals based on human genome research, and software for wireless devices were all popular with equity investors. These businesses were more likely than other new market areas to get venture capital and corporate funding. At that time investors were downgrading industrial equipment, new foods, and new car markets. As each kind of business became popular, others lost their opportunity for rapid funding. When you choose a market, you must also be ready to line up your support quickly to avoid becoming a victim of trends.

The other side of the coin is your existing support stream. If you have already received support from people and companies that invest in your core business, you may put them off by entering new and unknown markets. This investment is not merely financial. Others may invest time and people in your business—and these may be investments that you want to keep. Stressing new markets over proven businesses can make these investors nervous. To avoid this situation, be careful to sell the new market concept from the beginning. Don't assume that your investors will be supportive unless you work to convince them.

Hurdle 3: Assembling the Right Mix of Skills to Pull It Off

The effort of creating new markets requires new thinking. Some organizations are well tuned to that, but many are not. If every organization could do new thinking, Lockheed Martin would not have needed to set up its Skunkworks to identify breakthrough technologies; Mitsubishi Electric would not have chartered a separate division (VSIS, Inc., operated from 1996 to 2000) to try to compete with the U.S. chip companies; and IBM Corp. would not have needed to build an entirely different business structure to create the personal computer. Each of these companies recognized its organizational and people skill limits. They chose to go outside their normal corporate structures to bypass those limits.

Before you venture into new markets, you should make an honest assessment whether your team's ability to create is closer to Mitsubishi's or to Apple Computer's. Both are great organizations, but only one has a track record of new thinking and creating new markets.

Remember that your organization's sharply honed operational skills are not going to be as useful in new markets. Excellence in manufacturing, distribution, marketing, and delivery gives you critical competence in existing markets. To create new markets, though, you'll also need to find or build different skills.

Hurdle 4: Resisting the Siren Call of the Great Idea

The great idea is so very attractive. Gourmet meals delivered to your kitchen, the Apple Newton, movies-on-demand at home—all ideas that held so much promise to create new markets and sell millions. None worked. Just because you have a wonderful idea and can bring it to fruition doesn't automatically mean that you will succeed in creating a market. You face a real temptation, when creating a product, to assume that your invention is so cool that everyone will buy it. You may conclude that the very existence of your product will make a new market. After all, you love it, why won't everyone? It seems just so very obvious. It worked for Netscape's World Wide Web browser, why not for you?

Why do so many great ideas fail? Because the customers didn't find the results to be worth the trouble. Benefits are important, but you need problems to create new markets consistently. The key to clearing the hurdle is a problem that your customer considers to be important. When no one recognizes the problem, you have no market to create and dominate. Tang worked wonderfully as a drink for space travelers, but it was not a commercial success in homes. Tang provided a solution for which there is no problem.

Sometimes you don't need a problem to have success. After all, Pokémon ("Pocket Monsters" in Japan) and Furbys do not solve substantial problems. On the other hand, toy manufacturers produce thousands of great toy ideas that never make a profit. If you create a solution without a problem, you are working against the odds.

The proverbial advice is to build a better mousetrap so the world will beat a path to your door. Unfortunately, this only works if the world has mice, suffers from them, and really cares about that suffering. Thousands of communities in the world have great quantities of mice and rats but poor sales of mousetraps. We can easily make the mental connection that removing rats can help solve the problems of hunger and poverty. However, our ability to see a connection does not create a market in the customer's mind. Our understanding of the problem in a new market is usually incomplete. That brings us to the next hurdle.

Hurdle 5: Believing Expertise in an Old Market Equals Understanding in a New One

The difference between expertise in an established market and the expertise you'll need in a new market is difficult to recognize in everyday life. Your ability to succeed in the market you know can create blind spots when you look at markets that you do not know.

General Electric, Dow Jones & Company, IBM, and Sears were sure that they could create a general consumer or business market for what we now call Internet services. However, none of them could execute in a way that worked for the customers they had in mind. America Online found that model, but only after much larger companies had tried and failed. The market potential was there, but smart and competent people could not build the market.

Microsoft's domination in operating systems helped fund several attempts to become the market leader in the online market. Why the company needed to try so often is also interesting. In the early days of online communities, the company had the real opportunity to create and define a market. Early in the 1990s, Microsoft went to CompuServe, AOL, and Prodigy to talk about acquiring one of the new firms. Steve Case, president of AOL, recounted that he thought that the larger company could not see the right perspective. "When [Bill] Gates later noted that success in the online business was simply a 'software problem' that needed to be solved, the suggestion shocked Case. If Microsoft's vision of the online world was only about bits and bytes, there was little to talk about."[1] It was as though Microsoft could see things only through its own filters. The result? Microsoft tried several times to create the online market in the company's own view while then-small AOL became one of the largest media companies in the world.

The keys to success are in knowing how little your expertise will matter, in quickly finding the right expertise, and in planning to adapt quickly as you learn.

Hurdle 6: Realizing Your Friends and Customers May Not Know the Market

A California-based national consulting firm had made a name by solving problems for electrical utilities across the world. The CEO saw a new market in the coming deregulation of electrical power distribution in the United States. To take advantage of this opportunity, his firm was developing a product set that would help any utility learn to market in competitive environments. The product team had asked its favorite technical clients whether the need for such a product really existed. The firm's existing clients answered with an emphatic yes.

The question the CEO asked me was whether the team might be missing anything. After an hour of conversation, he changed only one part of the analysis effort. He called ten industry executives who were not friends or clients of the consulting firm. Eight of the ten said that they did not think the problem existed, and therefore they would not buy the solution. The CEO killed the project. The lesson he learned was to not just ask your friends. Instead, talk with people who will put their own interests ahead of yours. They are more representative of new markets.

Choosing Your Target—Time to Market Versus "Time to Market Acceptance"

The most critical resource that you have is time. Time never moves slowly for a business, and for one that wants to establish a new market, time moves much too quickly. C. Michael Armstrong had a vision of creating a new market in communications when he took over as CEO of AT&T Corp., one of the world's strongest companies. He was willing to bet the business on that new market, a risk the board accepted. Ultimately, AT&T failed. As Armstrong put it, "I knew coming in that my biggest enemy was time. My enemy hasn't changed."[2] For either the established business or a start-up, time has the highest priority. While most manufacturers focus on time to market, you should not make it your key concern for new markets. The reward is for being the first company to achieve "time to market acceptance" (a phrase coined by Regis McKenna, a Silicon Valley marketing consultant and author). Do not assume that simply being first to market will gain you dominance over that market. You need look no further than your word processing software for an example.

Today, Microsoft dominates the market for PC office software suites, and little is left for WordPerfect/Corel and IBM/Lotus to divide. Earlier, it was different. Before Windows became popular, WordPerfect was the dominant supplier of word processing software in the DOS market—so dominant that neither Microsoft (Word) nor IBM (DisplayWrite) could use their significant market presence to make an inroad with their offerings. As the first to market acceptance, WordPerfect won that contest and held a dominant position for years. Then a few things began to change.

The most critical change was that users started to move from DOS to the Windows operating system (OS). Although the overall Windows software was easier to use, no word processor worked well in Windows. Technically, this should have been an easy problem to solve. It became a business problem.

Although both WordPerfect and IBM had an advantage in market penetration with word processors, the companies were slow to invest in the Windows versions, and slow to garner acceptance on Windows. Microsoft worked assiduously to gain corporate customers. The company was not first to market, but it was first to gain market acceptance. Today Microsoft controls more than three-fourths of the market. The company and product that were first to market acceptance became the victor, even though they were not first to market.

Getting the Acceptance of the Right People

Deciding correctly whom you want to accept you is important. Acceptance by the media, consultants, and technical analysts will always be important. However, the approval of influencers is not enough to make the market happen. Acceptance by the users must always come first. The worst-case scenario occurs when you gain the acceptance of the wrong people. Integrated Services Digital Network (ISDN) is an example of a technology that many technical analysts touted very heavily. A standard for high-speed voice and data connections, ISDN was considered a requirement in new telecommunications products for years. Engagement consultants, who help U.S. customers choose equipment vendors, would commonly require ISDN capability before a system could be chosen. Vendors scrambled to design ISDN into their telephone systems and support hardware. The equipment suppliers and the influencers were almost unanimous in their support for the new technology. It seemed as though you could not be in the telecommunications equipment business without ISDN capability.

Influencers and suppliers were not enough. Customers, as a whole, remained unimpressed. ISDN became known as technology that "I Still Don't Need," and ISDN service never became popular. Acceptance by the analysts and media did not translate into acceptance by customers.

One of the most highly touted "firsts" in the Internet world was "push" technology. The media and analysts gave the concept glowing reviews. But the company that established itself as the standard for that idea hasn't converted market presence to economic success.

Push technology lets users choose what content they would like to get from the World Wide Web and have it continuously delivered (i.e., pushed) to them. Users just sign on and the information "channels" that they select flow across their computer screens when they are not actively running another application. Advertisers pay the cost to "buy eyeballs." The eyeballs represent more users, whom the advertisers hope to reach with their message. The market definer and leader was Pointcast.

Pointcast was successful in defining and dominating the market. The company signed up a quarter of a million new users per month for a period, making Pointcast a major success in delivering eyeballs to advertisers. Pointcast grew in clout and perceived value. In 1996, less than two years after the company distributed its first software, Pointcast was rumored to be negotiating its own sale to News Corp. for $450 million. Not bad for a company with a product it gave away at no cost.

Unfortunately for the company and the advertisers, even for a product that was "free," there was little in the equation for the customer. Users got updates on the news, but the service turned out to be fairly unimportant to most. With the updates many users also got reliability problems that far outweighed the advantages of bulletins. Many information services (IS) departments found it necessary to limit the use of Pointcast on corporate networks so that they could save network capacity for the business.

Push technology became a product viewed as good for advertisers but not for users. Companies with a message to push were accepting the concept, but they were the wrong market. The right market, customers (the "eyeballs"), was not accepting the concept. Soon, the number of people disconnecting the service started to exceed the number signing up. Advertisers could no longer count on a return. The economic equation started to fail. In 1999, the company sought support for an initial public offering that would have valued it at less than half the 1996 price. It was not well supported.[3] This company may have lost hundreds of millions of dollars in value in a very short time because it never achieved customer acceptance.

Old Economy or New?

You may have noticed that only a few of the products mentioned in this chapter are Internet-based offerings. The so-called new or Internet economy is an important part of the opportunity to create new markets, but the new economy is far from the complete opportunity.

From the perspective of creating and dominating new markets, the Internet is one of many valuable tools, but no more than a tool. As you look to new markets, do not assume that presence in the new economy guarantees you success or that the best path to prosperity comes via the Net or any electronic medium. Instead, look at the Net as you would look at a car. You need a vehicle to get somewhere, but the car may not be the right vehicle. Perhaps a plane would be better, or a dirt bike. The Internet may or may not be the right vehicle to launch your business into a new market. Don't let the vehicle become more important than the cargo or the destination.

The new economy will not replace the old one, any more than TV has replaced radio or than the Internet has replaced TV. You will find plenty of new markets left in the old economy. Remember, the potential for new markets relies on the perceived strength of the need, not the solution. Your two best sources for new markets development are:

▶Untapped and unrecognized needs of users

▶An acknowledged need without a solution

Do You Find or Create New Markets?

For better or worse, you rarely find a good new market. New markets are not an accidental result of random activity. New markets are the product of someone's recognizing a potential, finding the right solution, and bringing that solution to market in a way that works. It's difficult, demanding, and requires the greatest in creativity, marketing, engineering, and responsiveness. Consider this good news, because if new markets were easy, your competition would already be there. The rest of this book will give your team strategies and tools. You'll have to meld them together in a process that works for your unique business and the markets you choose. Then you can work to not only solve problems, but realize opportunities.

What Is the Potential for New Markets?

If you build new markets from undeveloped possibilities, how much possibility is there? The potential may develop to be either the untapped and unrecognized needs of a large group of users or an acknowledged need that demands a solution. Either way, a need signals that potential.

In Chapter 4 you'll look at how to uncover that need, but let's start with a frequent question: Are there still needs to meet? The fact is that you can find more burning needs than any of us can address in our lifetime.

Some of these needs are basic life essentials. The need for an HIV vaccine in developing countries is strong enough that the

U.S. National Security Council has identified it as a risk to this country. The need for replacement of chemical compounds that are less destructive to oxygen is real and urgent. A breakthrough in urban transportation may create a new market in what seems like an instant.

Some needs are leisure products that will do well in enhancing existing markets or creating new ones. In 2000, you saw a sudden market for Razor scooters with the wheels from inline skates. As a homeowner, I still feel the need for a squirrel-proof bird feeder.

The potential for new markets does not rely on the strength of the need. Look for the strength of the *perception* of the need. If you want to create a new market successfully, look for the perceived needs. Products as diverse as AZT, AOL, and the Land Camera were not accidents. You can repeat those successes for your own business.

2

Balancing Your Resources and Your Opportunities

How do you balance resource and opportunity? To succeed, what resources do you need to conserve and to invest wisely? You have three key resources to invest into opportunities. These are the three that you should conserve wherever you can.

Money is the first resource (or expense) that most managers mention. To create new markets you will need money. It may not require a great deal. Some very interesting markets happened on a low budget. Even on a tight budget, you need cash. However, as important as money is, it is not your key resource.

People are more important than money. Good people are hard to find and hard to keep. As hard as that task is, finding the right people gets harder when you decide to create and dominate new markets. People who are good at creating new markets are different from the ones who are good at improving your position in existing markets. You often need different people for initiating a market, and given the risks, you want only good people on your side. Whether you look for experience or are prepared to groom someone, you'll never have enough available.

The most important resource for your effort will be time. From the moment you decide to initiate a new market to the point when you decide to leave that market, you will be desperately short of time. When you have enough time, you can determine the pace of your work and, with the customers, the pace of the market. When you run short of time, you will never find enough people or money to overcome the gap. You will find yourself making decisions to spend money to save time and vice versa. As you will see in this chapter, to succeed in new markets you should conserve time over people, and both over money.

Another way to look at the cost of creating new markets is to look at opportunity costs. Every investment of a resource is a decision not to invest it somewhere else. That decision carries two risks. One is an obvious cost: that you will invest in market A and miss a bigger opportunity in market B. The second cost is less intuitive but even more dangerous to your success in new markets—namely, the risk that you will try to avoid that opportunity cost by investing in too many opportunities. That can cost you success in all of the new markets. This chapter explores these resource and opportunity issues.

Your First Resource: Money

Creating new markets is often expensive in dollars, but not every time. The cost of the new market is a function of two issues: the problem you are solving and the audience that feels that problem with the most intensity. Consumer markets are quite expensive; pharmaceutical or other regulated markets even more so. On the other hand, business markets can be concise and inexpensive to reach.

Chapter 1 discussed HIV vaccines as a market. The cost of entering such a market is measured in hundreds of millions of dollars. Figure 2-1 illustrates the investments made over eight years by VaxGen, Inc., the company that is furthest along in the development and test cycle for an HIV vaccine. (In the figure, year 1 through year 6 costs reflect real costs from 1995–2000; year 7 and 8 costs are projected investments for 2001–2002.) Other companies have spent similar amounts of money for similar vaccines. The research can be staggeringly expensive, and the testing can be beyond what many companies believe they can afford. On top of these costs, the process of working through regulations and governmental issues can absorb many more millions of dollars. The payoff for creating and dominating the mar-

Figure 2-1. Aggregate dollar cost of entering HIV vaccine market.

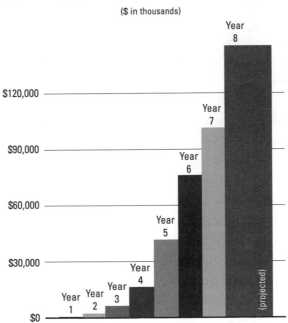

($ in thousands)

Sources: VaxGen and International AIDS Vaccine Initiative

ket will most likely be worth the cost, but that cost must somehow be borne to get you there.

The dollar cost to Chrysler for creating the market for minivans was $700 million This was more of a dollar risk than the company could afford without the support of loan guarantees. However, for a further comparison, consider Palm Computing and Federal Express. Even with several failures along the way, both companies created and dominated new markets with small initial investments.

For a few million dollars, a handful of engineers and marketers created a new market for handheld personal digital assistants (PDAs). Palm Computing was a small operation with comparatively low budgets until the company sold itself to U.S. Robotics. Over the next few years, U.S. Robotics and then 3Com invested tens of millions of dollars to increase the size of the company, but all that was based on a relatively small investment in the 1990s.[1] Palm's first prototype was a block of wood that the company's founder, Jeff Hawkins, carried in his shirt pocket. Hawkins and company cofounder Donna Dubinsky managed the company with very little money. More money would have been nice, but it wasn't required to create a new market.

The cost of creating a car market, as in the Chrysler example, is staggering. The cost of starting Federal Express was a pittance by comparison. For its investment FedEx Corp. got a new market: the reliable transfer of small but critical items overnight. Initially, Frederick Smith started Federal Express with the plan of helping the Federal Reserve move checks from city to city overnight. Using a great deal of leverage, Smith launched his effort to create a new market by investing $250,000 of his own money. With only that much cash, he acquired planes, commissioned detailed analyses from two consulting firms, hired staff, and built a great plan.[2] Federal Express adapted the plan several times and created a new market for overnight delivery. It was difficult, and the company nearly failed a number of times. However, the controlling factor for success was not the investment in money. For Fred Smith, people and time were even more critical.

Your Second Resource: People

Your company may have people who have excellent skills and instincts for getting the most revenue and share for existing markets. Usually, though, they are not the right skills for new markets. It may be tempting to ask people to take on both roles, but starting a new market effort with the wrong skills can cripple your work before you start.

Being the first company to sell cellular phones takes a leap of faith. Being the company that dominates the cellular phone market is an ongoing effort to make every detail a little better. In an existing market, you need a team that focuses on, and delivers, operational excellence.

Your marketing staff should be looking for an operational edge that allows you to segment a little better and perhaps price a little higher. Your manufacturing and delivery staffs should be looking to shave a few cents here and there, or offer a little more value for the same costs. In existing markets, the companies that compete with you may try to make your product appear to be the same as everyone else's, but at a higher cost. Your sales team has simultaneously to fight the commodity image and provide excellent service. Your finance team must look for little advantages to keep cash available. The chief financial officer (CFO) of one California software company has his firm making more money from investments than from its core product. The company is using that profit to subsidize expansion into new markets.

In existing markets, excellence is in the details. Creativity and imagination are not as important as understanding the business. In new markets, this model is reversed. Too much understanding of the old business can limit imagination, and that will limit the ability of your people to move the company into markets that do not yet exist. One key attribute of new markets is that they may not look like existing markets and may not respond to the same inputs as existing markets.

Abraham Maslow commented that to a man with a hammer, everything looks like a nail. To the designers who created the first handheld computer devices, it made perfect sense to downsize desktop computers to fit the smaller form factor. Their understanding of the old business dictated their view of the new opportunity. To Microsoft's managers, it made perfect sense to shrink Windows to fit that format. You could look at this as the ultimate extension of making computers more powerful. What used to take a roomful of hardware and special cooling units now fits in the palm of your hand. The view of the handheld computer was defined by the view of the room-size computer, and then the desktop and laptop computers. A logical conclusion, but the concept did not succeed. By the end of 2000, at least five companies had tried and failed to create a new market. That new market happened when a different team tried an approach that was not limited by their understanding of the old business.

The team at Palm Computing (now known as Palm, Inc.) challenged the "computer in your palm" view. They created something different. The development team chose to build an extension to a larger computer, not a replacement. Their concept was a creative jump that opposed the logic of the "experts" in the computer industry. In 2000, the new view held a commanding edge. While the growth of personal computer sales slowed to 10 percent, the market for handheld units doubled.[3] And, according to NPD Intelect, a research firm that tracks the handheld market, during this same time Palm's share of this new market (including all versions of the Palm operating system) increased from 78 percent to 86 percent. As in any successful new market effort, there are several contributing factors. Choosing people who were not limited by past views was a key contributor to Palm's ability to create a new market.

For operational excellence, choose people who learn well from the past. For new markets, choose people who also create well for the future. This attribute is not easy to specify when recruiting. You may find yourself authorizing highly nontraditional staffing alternatives. Making this choice happen is the responsibility of the general and line executives, not the human resources (HR) team.

Your Most Critical Resource: Time

The good news about people is that if you make a mistake when you hire a person, you can fix it within a few months or a year. If you make a mistake with your time, you do not have that luxury. Once that time is consumed, the most precious commodity in your world is gone forever.

The greatest expense for creating new markets is time. The effort takes time away from your core business (if you have one). It takes time away from other new market opportunities. It takes time away from your life and family.

Time is unique as a resource in another way; expending time will also cost you people and money. If you lose a month or a year, you may not gain any benefit, but you still have to find the funding to cover that period. Your best employees and partners will lose a little patience with you for that. If you lose too much time, these people may start to look elsewhere for more rewarding projects. The cost of time is additive. You have to add both people and money.

The search for a vaccine for HIV has been incredibly expensive for VaxGen. VaxGen was started by Genentech, Inc. and then spun off as a separate company in November 1995. Even after the initial $50 million investment by Genentech (which still owns the rights for manufacturing and distributing the drug AIDSVAX), VaxGen will spend $132 million and dedicate seventy people to the effort to bring AIDSVAX through the tests that will prove whether it works. If the vaccine works, it will have been tested only on some varieties of the HIV virus.

As difficult as it may be to find this much money for a highly speculative venture, when the company talks to investors it stresses the investments in time, not money. From the inception of the project in 1995 to first applying for regulatory approval, VaxGen has laid out a timeline of more than seven years. This is not time to invent and develop the initial product—that work was mostly done by Genentech between 1992 and 1995. The seven years do not include time to get Food and Drug Administration (FDA) permission to market the product, or time to market the product and gain acceptance. The seven years are time to prepare and to test. VaxGen has no slack time in the schedule.

The risk here is worth noting. VaxGen is living, effectively without revenue, on a consumption rate of $20 million to $25 million per year. This involves seventy employees, generally highly trained people who could find work in profitable companies. The company is investing seven years to prove an idea. At the end of the period, VaxGen may or may not have a successful vaccine. Either way, the company will still not have begun serious marketing. At the end of testing, AIDSVAX will not yet be approved by the governments of the United States and Thailand (the two countries where clinical trials are being conducted). VaxGen cannot market the vaccine without that approval. If the tests produce poor results, approval may be difficult and the investment of years, people, and money will not create a new market for many more years. If ever.

In an ideal world, VaxGen would have unlimited funds for development and access to as many good people as it needs. The question is whether this would improve the chances of success. Could VaxGen trade money for time?

Don Francis, the president of VaxGen, has answered that question by saying "You need three doses of the vaccine. You need six months to start" before you can really test. Unlike a treatment, the testing team can't demonstrate success until the patients are free of illness for a period of time. Adding money does not shorten that time.[4]

The result is reflected in Frederick Brooks's comment that "the bearing of a child takes nine months, no matter how many women are assigned."[5] Unlimited funds may shrink VaxGen's testing work from seven years to six, but no further. Key parts of creating a new market must follow a sequence for VaxGen or any other vaccine creator. Success, as defined by getting a product through testing and into the approval cycle, will take this many years.

Success, however, is also defined as being the first HIV vaccine to gain market acceptance. VaxGen cannot cut years from the schedule. It cannot afford to add them, either. If VaxGen takes too long to get to success, the company runs several key risks. One is resources. If the company stalls, people will leave, money will run short, and investors will abandon the effort. Another risk is being beaten by other companies. Many firms (perhaps thirty) are vying for that market. Some have substantial subsidies. None of them can go faster than VaxGen at full speed, but if VaxGen slows, the company could be scooped at the last minute. There are lots of clocks for VaxGen to race against. The company cannot afford to waste time.

How Do You Measure Time as a Resource?

Time is best measured as the time it takes to meet a specific objective, and the right one at that. For instance, "time to market" is too vague a term. Do you mean time to first brochure (as has been practiced by several software companies)? Time to initial beta shipment? Time to general release? Time to customer acceptance? Time to a certain volume?

The difference between these measurement points is immensely important. In the handheld PDA market that Palm now dominates, Casio, Inc., or Psion PLC may have been the first to ship brochures and then product. Apple Computer was probably the first company to ship PDAs in volume, eventually selling perhaps a half million units. However, Palm was the first product to achieve customer acceptance. The company's volumes—more than 10 million Palm brand handhelds by the end of the year 2000—far outstripped all the other vendors combined.

The late Malcolm Forbes, Jr., a man who lacked very little, was reportedly asked what he wished for. His answer: "More time." Time is a strategic asset when you want to create a market. When you can move quickly to market acceptance, you can shorten the time to domination of that market. That gives you the opportunity to move into the next new market effort. Many efforts fail, some succeed, but the sooner you get to the level of market acceptance, the better.

The successes make it easier to see the failures. With that vision, you can get out of a poor situation more quickly. One of the hardest decisions for managers is knowing when it's time to leave the market. Spending too long in a failing market swallows time, people, and money that could be better invested in the future. Owners and managers stay when they don't know when to call it quits, when another few months or investments will not be enough to turn the corner.

Your best way to know when to stop a new market effort is from experience. The more success you see, the easier it will be to recognize efforts that are going to fail. When you can forecast failure correctly, you can quickly cut off the investments of time, people, and money into a losing proposition. The sooner you leave a failing new market, the sooner you can manufacture your next opportunity.

Time can be a significant barrier to new competition. When you are able quickly to move to new markets, quickly establish domination, and quickly move on, other companies must speed up to your pace to compete. America Online (AOL) used this advantage successfully to establish a new market before IBM, Sears, CompuServe, GE, and other, smaller companies could get mobilized.

Lessons Learned About Time as a Resource: AOL

In the fall and winter of 1993, AOL started to distribute software disks through direct marketing. Starting with magazine "out-serts," the company moved to distribution via airlines, direct mail, handouts at book and appliance stores, and almost any other way the marketing team could think to give software disks away. For a year or two, the joke was that no one had to buy floppy disks anymore. If you needed a disk, all you had to do was to wait for it to arrive in the mail from AOL.

The plan was to make AOL easy to install and use and to increase the product's brand awareness among consumers. In the first tests, AOL hoped it might get a good response to the magazine and direct mail distribution. In direct marketing, 1 percent is usually considered a good rate of response, and half of that is acceptable. AOL started to get 10 percent response rates. These results were too obvious not to be noticed. The only question was how long it would take for AOL's competitors to respond. Time became a critical resource for AOL in two ways.

The first was protecting a market lead. As AOL was carpet bombing the country with disks, the marketing director who initiated and ran the program worried about "going to direct marketing hell, but we needed to get to a critical mass in the fastest way we could, so no one could blow us over." Every day she expected a response from Prodigy and CompuServe, but the other companies were slow to reply in kind. "It was like a blessing from heaven every minute that went by and that didn't happen."[6]

Simultaneously, this presented a tremendous challenge to the technical team at AOL. In 1993, the company used a system design that could handle only 8,217 simultaneous users. As the direct marketing worked, AOL's marketing machine ramped up to distribute even more disks. For every hundred disks the company distributed, ten new users would sign up and start to use the service. The faster marketing worked, the faster user demands ramped up.

Increasing the overall number of users eventually translated to more users who wanted to be online simultaneously. For every thousand users, an online service could expect thirty to be actively using the system simultaneously. (The ratios have changed with the arrival of high-speed digital subscriber lines.) AOL's systems could handle only a relatively small number of users at once. As the marketing worked, simultaneous users were being added even more quickly. The technical teams had less and less time to expand capacity. This restriction was firm. When the total number of subscribers passed 274,000, the design limit would be reached and AOL's systems would start to fail. The day that the total number would reach 274,000 was approaching more and more quickly.

If the company added infinite funding and unlimited numbers of people, it could not buy more time to stretch the hard limit of 8,217 simultaneous users. Time ran out in February 1994, and the service started to fail.

The time issue was magnified by the expectations of the new medium. AOL users (and new computer users, in general) are used to immediate responses from their computers. By failing to give quick access to the service, AOL failed to meet expectations. The company encountered an uproar.

On the other hand, time was an asset for marketing. Assuming that the universe of potential members would be limited, AOL could use time to create a barrier to entry for Prodigy and CompuServe. This barrier to entry would be constructed as America Online signed up members who might have gone to the other companies. The more sign-ups, the fewer new users would be available for the other companies. This enlarged the obstacle to the success of those other companies.

AOL faced substantial risk. Among computer aficionados, slow response time is often acceptable. If members of that community know that they are testing something new, they are likely to be tolerant of new product failures. Consumer product companies do not have that advantage. Consumers expect their products to work from the first time they are installed. Their expectation is that the product will work as advertised.

AOL's marketing emphasized that ease of use. This increased the number of members who joined as it increased their expectations for easy access to the network. However, AOL was having great difficulty meeting those expectations. The risk was not just short-term unhappiness among members. If the members did not have a satisfactory experience in their first few days, they might unsubscribe immediately. That could result in lost opportunity to create the new market. A few years later, a similar problem resulted in a series of lawsuits. The time to correct the problem before it started faded as AOL marketing did its job. The time to correct the problem after it started was virtually nil, because the service could not afford to upset many of its new members.

Balancing Opportunity Costs— Can VaxGen Create a Market?

One way to reduce risk is to spread the investment among many opportunities—a common strategy. With many CEOs, the tendency is to be accidentally or intentionally opportunistic. These executives and owners are willing to jump to the next big thing and quickly change one opportunity for a better one. While this strategy was quite obvious in the dot-com companies in the late 1990s, the tendency to act opportunistically has been with us for decades. The question is, when can that tendency hurt more than it helps?

To look at a case of balancing opportunity costs with resources and risks, consider again the example of VaxGen. This company has invested considerable resources into a market that does not exist—vaccines for HIV. The opportunity is immense; so is the expense in time, people, and money resources.

When Drs. Don Francis and Robert Nowinski founded Vax-Gen, jumping from one opportunity to another was not an option they ever considered. The lack of option was not technical, it was a conscious business and personal decision. The two founders made a commitment to ignore other opportunities and conserve resources.

VaxGen's vaccine technology is both unusual and powerful. Medically, the process can be used beyond HIV. The techniques offer promise in treating such widely spread diseases as hepatitis B or genital herpes and perhaps even breast cancer. For many CEOs, the temptation would be to allocate time, people, and money to several of these opportunities. That temptation could be very strong for VaxGen. The risk in its current business strategy is immense. The whole company is based on the success of two products based on one technology. That technology has to be approved by government agencies that are not known for speed or leniency. To get to approval, the company has had to raise nearly $150 million and will spend almost all of it to get there. The time and people are even more expensive. The company, including early development from Genentech, will have invested a decade of time, and now dozens of people, to get to the start of the approval process. If the new technology fails to operate as planned, or if the tests fail for any of many reasons, the investment is dead.

For many CEOs, this would be an argument to spread into multiple opportunities. The founders of VaxGen balanced opportunity cost with resources and did not choose the path of multiple opportunities. Don Francis later said, "If you look at different opportunities—this was such a huge endeavor that if we diluted this . . . [we faced the real possibility of failure]. Why? The immensity of this job."[7] Conducting a trial of 8,000 patients on two continents is a major undertaking, and for any company there are only so many good people and so much time to invest. As noted previously in this chapter, that time is not very flexible. If VaxGen wastes time by stretching too thin, it runs the substantial risk of losing the opportunity to a larger competitor.

A second reason to walk away from other opportunities was "the financial support. When it came to financing [VaxGen] went to simplicity." Most of the people and firms Francis and Nowinski approached for funding felt more comfortable if there was only one area of focus: HIV. Expanding the research to include the treatment of other diseases increases the risk of failing in all areas, so many financial sources argued for a single effort. The reasoning—for the management and development teams to put all their eggs in one basket—makes it easier to manage the risk. It also makes the teams less likely to lose focus.

This is the opportunity cost, and with vaccines that cost is even higher than with most products. "The downside is the binary nature of this work," says VaxGen's Francis. "New vaccines take years" to prove out. "Vaccines are much riskier" than treatments. The reason is that when you test a treatment, you use sick patients, and you get quick feedback. They either improve or regress in a short period of time. "With HIV treatments, you can measure T-cells or viral load in a few weeks."

With a vaccine, you are testing healthy patients, waiting for them to get ill. If you are successful, you don't know it for months or years. As well, the number of patients that you enroll needs to be much higher. For a powerful anti-HIV, drug pharmaceutical companies might test on a few hundred people. Francis says that for AIDSVAX (VaxGen's product), "I have to go to 8,000 people."

A third reason to pay a higher opportunity cost is access to people. When you ask Dr. Francis what drove this focus, he will tell you "more importantly, this is what we wanted to do. We wanted to do it. [Stopping] HIV is the big gun." The VaxGen team has a sense of mission. As with Apple developing the Macintosh computer, a sense of mission can be critical to attracting the best candidates. Diffusing the mission with multiple opportunity goals can make you less desirable as an employer. In a tight labor market, VaxGen gets the right candidates calling the company. Francis thinks that this is partially due to the tight focus of the company's mission. It may seem counterintuitive, but increasing opportunity cost can increase your ability to recruit the right people. The balance is that opportunities spread risk, but willingness to pay opportunity cost is a good way to gain and conserve your critical resources.

The opportunity cost is also balanced against risk. VaxGen's risk is very high. As the World Bank suggested, "HIV vaccine is a market failure." The supply and demand forces are disconnected. The greatest need for the vaccine is in those countries that are least able to pay for it. A product that costs dollars per dose, even if it only requires a few doses, is out of the price range of many countries, as dramatically illustrated in Figure 2-2.

Creating a product that your customer cannot afford is a risky proposition.

Going into the last five years of vaccine development and trials, VaxGen faced this issue. "We were assuming that there is

Figure 2-2. The countries with the most need for a vaccine have the least ability to pay for it.

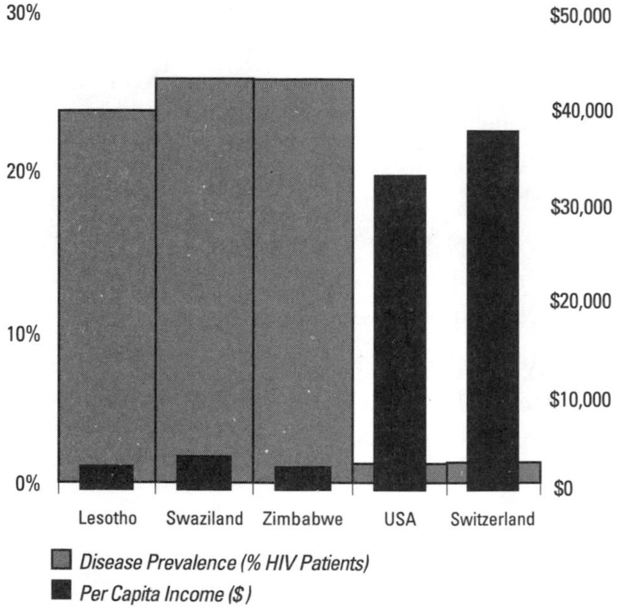

Disease Prevalence (% HIV Patients)
Per Capita Income ($)

Sources: World Bank, World Health Organization

a market failure, with the presumption that it would need to be fixed," says Francis. If it is not fixed shortly after the vaccine is approved for use, VaxGen could still fail.

VaxGen does have a plan to create this market, and it resembles an odd sort of channel strategy. In this model, nongovernmental organizations become the channel. Nonprofit organizations such as the Bill & Melinda Gates Foundation will buy the vaccine at dollars per dose and provide them to impacted countries at a cost of pennies per dose or less.

Nevertheless, even that does not eliminate the risk. The glib comment is that selling a vaccine to sub-Saharan Africa is like selling food in Ethiopia. This analogy is unfortunately accurate. During the famine, the infrastructure to move food to Ethiopians was inadequate for the task. The infrastructure to move vaccine dosages to needy people in less developed countries may also be inadequate. It can come down to as simple an issue as needles. If the HIV vaccine requires a needle, and there are not enough, healthcare workers will have to share needles to administer the vaccine. Every case of needle sharing increases the risk of transmitting a multitude of diseases. Sharing needles can create more damage than the vaccine would avoid. If the vaccine works but there are no needles, VaxGen does not have a market in those countries.

Relying on developed nations to be new markets is attractive, but the developed nations have their own risk from economic imbalance. In the United States and other wealthy nations, insurance companies will pay for coverage for sick people, but they often won't pay for the vaccine that would prevent the sickness. This has a chilling effect on the vaccine market as a whole. When a well-funded pharmaceutical company compares opportunity costs, the equation makes it difficult for an internal manager to champion a new market creation. For the amount of time, people, and money resources it takes to create a new market, the company could test several new treatments in existing markets.

Time is still a critical resource. A new drug treatment for HIV may come to market a year or two faster than a vaccine. Governments and insurance companies are the largest customers of both products, and they have limited budgets. For the drug companies, it is often easier to sell products that treat or cure a small number of people instead of preventing the illness in a large number. Since treatments have a shorter approval cycle and are easier to sell, they get a greater share of the resources inside pharmaceutical companies. Projects to create vaccines are measured against opportunity costs, and often lose.

Opportunity cost in part explains why VaxGen exists as a separate company. As Francis puts it, "Why spin [VaxGen] out of Genentech? Because I cannot compete with their products when I am inside the company." It is often seen as easier to compete in existing markets than it is to create new ones, to create a product that you know will sell and enter a market that you understand. The opportunity cost is not just other vaccines. If you invest in an HIV vaccine, you are paying opportunity costs for a whole series of other, easier-to-sell treatments and drugs.

Why bother to take the risks and to bypass all the opportunities? Francis suggests two logical answers: altruism and greed (shown graphically in Figure 2-3).

On the one hand, as expressed by the vertical axis in Figure 2-3, you have the inestimably important mission of creating a vaccine that can help stop AIDS from destroying countries and destabilizing the power structure of continents.[8] The team that succeeds here will have done a great deed. Following the horizontal axis, the company that succeeds may be able to create two new markets, one quite lucrative and one that delivers volume but not high margins.

Figure 2-3. Altruism versus greed.

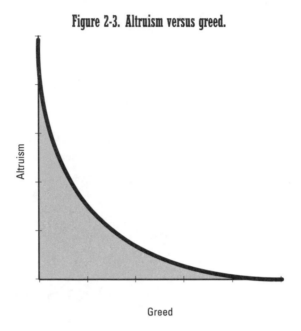

Greed

In the early stages of getting support for VaxGen, Don Francis would talk about both altruism and greed as reasons to develop the vaccine. As he drew the altruism versus greed chart, Francis would say that he did not care which brought an investment in VaxGen, as long as the investment occurred. He modified this statement after a banker pointed to the altruism axis and said, "I don't know anybody here." The upside for this work is high—high enough that many bankers and individuals have invested in the opportunity.

Competition is a major concern when you evaluate opportunity costs, and that works in favor of the new market. When you face competition, it affects margins and market share. You have to adapt your business plans accordingly. This is less of an issue if you are creating a new market, because you have no competition from other companies. For VaxGen, Francis notes that "the competition is with the bug." That is true today, but if the company makes a mistake and loses a few years, another company could catch and pass it. With around thirty other projects to develop an HIV vaccine, time is a crucial advantage and resource to Francis's team. By walking away from opportunities, VaxGen is staying in the competition to beat the bug and reap the rewards.

Opportunity Costs and New Markets

Every moment, person, and dollar that you invest in a new market is unavailable for other opportunities. Opportunities are not a resource, but they cost you access to resources. In 1994, AOL was struggling to digest its success. During that period, Prodigy and CompuServe could have made an opportunity for themselves. If one of the two companies had aggressively courted unhappy AOL users, it could have made a difference.

VaxGen's investment in time, people, and money is costing the company many other opportunities. That same phenomenon happens with much larger companies. When Merck or GlaxoSmithKline invests in the HIV vaccine opportunity, it has to bypass possible investments in other new markets. If VaxGen gets to the market first and can dominate it, those other opportunities will also be gone. Merck and GlaxoSmithKline will have missed the HIV vaccine market as well as other markets.

Opportunity cost is a primary reason that VaxGen is not planning to sell and market its primary product. The company has the choice of investing time, people, and money either to develop HIV vaccines for other strains of the virus or to build a delivery infrastructure. VaxGen has chosen to trade the opportunity for profits (from owning manufacturing and delivery) for the opportunity to build more vaccines. The process to develop marketing and sales teams would take time, people, and money that would divert VaxGen from the company's primary opportunities.

The potential rewards are quite large. If Genentech and VaxGen form a partnership to produce and deliver the first HIV vaccine, they have the opportunity to enter a market of a half billion dosages per year or more. To get to that kind of chance, Genentech has also missed other opportunities. That company once had the rights to Epogen and Neupogen, two of the most successful biotech drugs ever.

Creating and dominating markets is a high-reward, high-risk game. VaxGen, America Online, Federal Express, and Palm Computing all passed up opportunities in order to get to the one that each company believed would work. For VaxGen and for others, it pays to limit opportunities. Choosing the right opportunity is the critical step, and that starts with investing your critical resources into solving the right problem.

3

It's the Problem That Matters

You don't find new markets. New markets do not exist until someone creates them. When you ask a team of people to go find a new market for your product, you are giving them the wrong instructions. The instructions should be to create a new market, and the difference between those two words—*find* versus *create*—will be important to you.

One reason so few new markets are created is that most companies focus on the solutions that they make—the products that they are already selling. They miss new market opportunities by trying to find matches for products to which they are already committed. This leaves a considerable amount of room for companies that choose to create new markets by looking at problems, not products. Your real opportunity is in problems.

New Markets Are Created from Potential

If new markets do not yet exist, where are they? New markets exist in potential. The creation of a new market occurs at the convergence of perceived need with acceptable solution in a way that did not previously exist. That phrase, "did not previously exist," is part of what makes it difficult for some people and companies to succeed in creating new markets. It is the difference between finding existing markets and creating new ones. For example:

Find	Create
Some managers find the right answers from defined solutions.	Others create new solutions.
Finding is faster.	Creating and testing (to see if the creation works) is slower.
One finds ways to make a product at a lower cost . . .	. . . but another creates a new market.

Finding the right answer is an important skill. Just look at your best managers. They have been trained to sort through pre-existing options. Then they identify the correct alternative and quickly and correctly implement that choice. Many great cooks work this way too, searching the kitchen and then finding the right combination of flavors and condiments to make the "solution" that they want.

Creating is a different skill. Managers who create well have been trained (or have trained themselves) to look for a solution that did not exist before they started. Cooks who create will leave the known ingredients and techniques and experiment with flavors and foods that have no history. The creative person is not looking to find what is available, but to build something new. Creating the first commercial web browser was not a function of finding the components and assembling them well. Federal Express was not founded on or built from existing ideas. The core idea was created afresh. The instant camera market was not a line extension. Edwin Land's camera was a creation from new ideas as well as old. None of these new markets was there to be found; each was created.

As the AOL online version of the *New Oxford Dictionary of English* would have it, when the cook creates he or she brings something into existence. This is in the sense of creating "form out of nothing."[1] To a certain extent, it is the difference between predestination and authority of self. You may discover ways to make a product at a lower cost, but you would create a new market.

Occasionally, you will find a manager or executive who will state that there's nothing new in the world. This thought process can be perfect for operational excellence because it streamlines the search for quick and effective solutions. However, a person who says that nothing new exists in the world is effectively saying that creating is not possible. This can be a useful attitude for a manager who has responsibility for a process whose essence should not change. Nonetheless, a manager or owner who works on that principle cannot create new markets. The process of creating new markets is the process of identifying and satisfying potential. Potential new markets are not waiting for you and your business to find them. They are waiting to be brought into existence.[2]

Like the cook in the kitchen, you must be willing to accept more risk and different results when you create. Cooks who are truly creative make some disastrous meals. Finding cooks who can create wonderful disasters is difficult. Stomaching the costs is even harder. Although you can quickly clean up a cook's mistakes, there is more at risk from a mistake in creating a new market. To reduce the costs of time, people, and money, it makes sense to look for common denominators for success. One of those denominators is the convergence of the right forces. When that happens (see Figure 3-1), the market can be created.

The first arrow in Figure 3-1 is the high level of need, as perceived by the customer. Identifying that need is the key to a successful new market. Without that need, you risk having a solution looking for a problem, which usually fails. What, then, is the way to find the need?

Figure 3-1. Both forces must come together to create a new market.

The Potential Is in Problems

Let's start with the assumption that markets are an economic structure. They perform the function of trading one product, service, or currency for another. Each product, service, and currency has a value. What you want in new markets is to build the combination of products or services that has the highest possible value—value to the customer, not just to the provider. This can be shown as an equation:

$$X \times P/S = \text{Value}$$

where *P/S* means product (or service) and *X* is the multiplier that we try to create.

The traditional way to start this equation is to start with the product and make it better and better. This method results, often, in a product in search of a problem to solve. For example, consider some of the dot-com companies that came into existence in the 1990s or some consumer products in grocery stores.

Webvan provides an excellent example of a company that tried to create a new market, dominate it, and then turn that market into profits. The founders of the company identified a niche that no one had entered—delivery of groceries ordered from the Web. They quickly built the infrastructure to provide that service. In an informal survey, their target customers indicated they were very attracted to the service and valued it highly.

The company did things right when it came to taking care of the customer. If you placed an order, the company let you decide when you wanted your groceries delivered. Webvan provided fresh meats, produce, and high-quality nonperishables. The drivers delivered to your home, even if they had to climb three flights of stairs to do it. Webvan prices were competitive and ordering was simple. Delivery was free if you bought a reasonable minimum. Selection of brands and products was good. (Webvan experimented with the selection and free delivery models as the company worked to balance profitability with service, but kept them acceptable to most of their core customers.) For the same cost as driving to the store and standing in line, Webvan delivered the food to you. Doing well by the customer, and with no serious competition in its markets and an excellent infrastructure, Webvan should have provided a winning solution. Instead, in 2001 it ran out of cash and closed.

Quadraphonic sound was the next great thing in consumer music in the 1970s. By adding more signals and hardware that could separate two stereo signals into four signals, suppliers of these systems created a real sense of surround sound in the home. You could listen to Emerson, Lake, and Palmer or to a Beethoven concerto and feel as if you were in a concert hall. Getting that sound required new stereo equipment in your home. It also required that you buy LP records that would feed the correct signals to your new hardware. If you wanted that sense of reality, this technology could deliver it for you. Not enough people wanted it, and the idea failed.

Integrated Services Digital Network (ISDN) provides an example of a business-to-business product and service that made excellent sense to the providers. When it works, it allows the telephone companies to deliver uniform and moderately high speed data service to any consumer or company in the area that has telephone wires. For a small (at least that was the idea) investment, the phone companies could provide several high-speed voice and data connections to every home over a single pair of wires. Using existing wires, the same phone companies could provide two voice or data circuits to every user in a business, over a single pair of wires per user.

Putting several voice or data conversations on a single pair of wires represented a tremendous savings by allowing the telephone companies to avoid difficult infrastructure investments. As people added faxes and computer connections to their homes and offices, the telephone companies could add hardware and software to their central offices to support the new features and avoid the difficult, cash-intensive, and very time-consuming tasks of digging up wires, pulling new cables, and negotiating rights-of-way. The cost per connection for ISDN was high, but that cost could be passed to the consumer without a large cost per connection to the supplier. ISDN was a great deal for the suppliers, but not so good for the users. It never took off in North America.

Webvan, quadraphonic sound, and ISDN are all solutions that made great sense to the companies providing these products and services. Yet, none of the three solutions lived up to its commercial promise. The customers stayed away in droves. They were great solutions that did not sell well. Why? Because they are solutions without problems. Webvan's prospective customers didn't feel strongly that they had a problem to be solved. Stereo buyers did not feel a need for a quadraphonic system. Many voice and data customers came to the conclusion that ISDN stood for "I Still Don't Need" it.

Selling Pain to Create Markets

The current business literature is rife with companies that had a great solution but no problem. It is equally populated with companies that solved the wrong problem.

In the 1970s, there was a spate of lawsuits targeting retail stores that did not do enough to prevent slippery floors. The problem is quite straightforward—if you are a grocery store, you water your produce to keep it fresh and appealing. When you do that, you may leave a puddle on the floor. Customers can slip and hurt themselves. If they slip and hurt themselves, they can sue with a suggestion of negligence. One lawsuit, even if you defend successfully, can cost hundreds of thousands or even millions of dollars in legal fees and other expenses. A product that would prevent these suits would be solving a real problem.

Such a product was introduced, a coating that you could add to your floors and make them less slippery. It would also soften the floor (an advantage to the staff that walks it all day long and to the customers who did fall) but not slow shopping carts. This "coating in a paint can" was designed to be easily installed and was inexpensive to maintain. For a few thousand dollars a store, the owners could coat the floors of the produce sections and be sure of a much-reduced risk of lawsuits. The solution would pay for itself the first time that a customer did not fall.

In a vacuum, this would be an easy financial decision. However, storeowners do not work in a vacuum. They have hundreds of places where they need to invest time and money and dozens of more immediate problems than "slip and fall" lawsuits. When having to decide whether to invest in a floor coating or a new refrigerator case, the refrigerator case would win because its need is more immediate. The owner would see it as a more critical need.

In the end, the floor coating did not survive. The product did not solve a problem that the storeowner saw as important enough, as painful as it may be to have a customer fall and sustain an injury on your premises.

To avoid the history of the floor coating, you can go in one of three directions:

1. Create so much pain that a market has to exist. It can be done, but this strategy requires considerable resources and organization.[3]

2. Make the problem you already solve seem to loom larger. Making the problem seem larger is the most common strategy. It works for awhile.

3. Find out what problems are already looming large to your customers.

Sales training usually focuses on the pain of a problem. Some courses teach the salespeople to make more pain or to amplify the pain as much as possible. In this philosophy, you would create the floor coating and then go to the stores and talk about the costs of lawsuits. A good salesperson might even go so far as to demonstrate a slip and fall in the store. He would then follow up with a cite from a torts case where the defendant (a different store) lost a great deal of money or time from the suit. This might be enough to sell a fair amount of coating.

The problem with pain-based marketing is that pain does not overwhelm larger problems for any substantial length of time. The customer quickly begins to compare the pain of the issue you raise with the pain of other problems. As critical as the floor issue may be, the store manager will often place priority on a problem, such as power costs or speed of cash registers, that she really feels. You can't replace that other pain for an extended period. You may make a sale, but not keep the customer. The most important pain will always win. This strategy won't help you create and then dominate a new market.

The second strategy is to start with that most important pain. In the grocery business, an overall margin of 2 percent is large. Anything that threatens that operating sales margin is a real source of pain. If you find out that the customer is more concerned with margins than with lawsuits, addressing the margin issue may bring you more success.

The problem you face may be that you have already created a floor coating before you find the real pain issue. This happens when companies decide that either they:

▶Know more than the customers, or

▶Do not need to ask customers what they perceive as real problems

Having a solution with the wrong problem doesn't mean that you should sell harder. It means that you made a mistake in defining the problem. If you truly want to deliver a service, fix that fundamental mistake by looking at the problems that keep your customer awake at night.

What Is a Good Problem to Solve?

Once you decide that you don't want to have a solution in search of a problem, you must start looking at problems to solve. However, not all problems are created equal, and not all solutions are going to be equally valuable. The key to success in creating and dominating a new market is to identify the right problems to solve.

The right problem is relative. Consider your list of priorities for the week. Do you have more than two or three problems on it waiting to be solved? As many as a dozen or more? Most managers and owners respond emphatically yes.

How you rank these problems is individual; some are at the top of your list, some at the bottom. If a vendor comes to you and credibly offers to fix the tenth problem, will you want to hear about it? Probably, yes. If a different vendor comes to you and credibly offers to fix the second or third most important problem, which vendor will you listen to first?

Most owners and managers will give more attention to the solution that addresses the problem that is at or near the top of the list. Why invest scarce resources in the least important problems if you can invest them in the most important ones?

If you want successfully to create a new market, you will find your efforts competing for the same scarce resources among customers. They will evaluate your solution against their problem, and if the problem is important enough they will assign time, people, and money to making the problem go away. The question is whether the problem is important enough to the customer. If not, what should you do?

One possible answer is to try and make it more important. Through positioning, advertising, good sales technique, and sometimes through creating fear, you have many opportunities to elevate the customer's perception of how critical the problem can be. This path allows the solution to be more important than the problem. This sort of thing is what gives advertising a bad name. Artificially building importance is expensive in terms of the time, people, and money it takes, and it does not always work. Deodorant sells today because advertising has increased the level of concern people have about the problem. Tang drink powder, by contrast, does not sell in large quantities. Creating a problem is a difficult path.

A second answer is to look for the problem that is at the top of your customers' list. If data users did not care about putting multiple conversations on one pair of wires, what did they care about? The founders of Palm Computing (today Palm, Inc.) thought that it might be to put the data in a person's hand instead on the phone. Palm products have sold much better than ISDN.

Is Money the Right Problem?

A frequent assertion from sales teams is that "price is always an issue" in selling both low-cost and expensive products. How often do you get requests to discount before the proposal is even submitted?

Financial arguments commonly dominate the benefits section of a business-to-business proposal. Often, a marketing or sales team will emphasize cost savings as the reason to buy their product. When I work with sales management, I frequently hear the complaint that the customer did not buy, although the product would pay for itself within a year or two. The operating assumption, then, is that saving money is the problem to be solved. If the product will reduce your costs, you will buy it; any rational person would.

That argument is logical, but it doesn't work that way in the real world. Saving money is a solution that is often addressing a low-level problem. Return on investment (ROI) is a broadly held concern. ROI goes well beyond cost control to include revenue and operational issues. Almost all companies have it on their list of issues (1990s Internet companies aside). However, the question is not whether it is broadly held, but whether it is high on the list of problems to be solved.

When our consulting firm, The Meyer Group, asked CEOs to tell us their top problems, one of the interesting results was that the top problems were often not financial. With senior executives, improving cost controls or saving money is not going to get you success. When asked to identify the problems that keep them awake at night, CEOs repeatedly identified two issues:

1. Creating and dominating new markets

2. Finding and keeping the best people[4]

Neither of these challenges is easily measured by money. While the presence and level of profits will certainly be a yardstick for overall success, many top problems that you can solve will be measured by softer criteria. ROI does not rank highly here. If you want to create a market that requires the attention of the top executive, solving an ROI problem will not get you the same response from your target audience as helping the business to create and dominate new markets.

That applies to the long-term issues for owners and general managers, but what about the rest of the business?

What Are the Top Problems for Operational Management?

If you are going to look for problems that need to be solved by businesses, you may do best simply to ask your prospective customers. In the spring of 2001, The Meyer Group conducted a wide-ranging e-mail survey to ask that question.[5] Our intent was not to discover the core problems on which to build a market. We wanted to find out where cost control ranks among the list of problems to manage.

This is a business-to-business discussion. If you want to create a new market focused on consumers, the answers will not be the same. However, the trends and lessons will be important for consumer markets as well.

The survey covered 400 managers, directors, vice presidents, and chief executive officers in the United States. We asked each respondent to tell us his or her title and then identify the top two operational problems that day. Not everyone took the time to respond. Of those managers who did answer, there were a very high proportion of senior executives. More than two-thirds of the respondents are at the vice president level or above, with almost half being CEOs or the equivalent (see Figure 3-2).

The survey was conducted in the spring of 2001, during a unique period of unsettled economic news. The United States was dancing close to recession. Many companies that had counted on continued growth were overextended. Dot-com and technology stock valuations were crashing, and many high-flying companies were heading to unprofitable quarters. In Silicon Valley, layoffs were starting in businesses that had never laid off an employee. It was traumatic to many managers and executives, and some high-profile executives focused on the change to the economy at great length. The president of Cisco Systems, a leading network company, donated his annual salary so that three employees could avoid the layoff. Given that, you might expect an emphasis on cost-control issues. This survey yielded the unexpected.

The most common operational issues identified by respondents were day-to-day functional problems; this grouping was

Figure 3-2. Top operational problems survey—respondents.

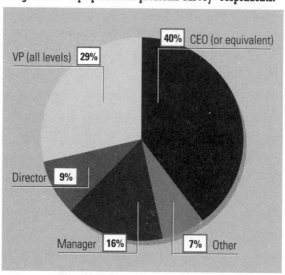

More than 3/4 of those who answered were executives.
Total is greater than 100 percent due to rounding.

followed closely by revenue and market positioning issues (examples of both are given in the next sections). Communications and people issues came next, followed distantly by information technology (IT) issues. Only 1 percent of respondents identified controlling costs as one of their top two operational concerns (see Figure 3-3).

To understand the lessons of the survey, it helps to look more closely at who responded and what functional and revenue issues they detailed.

As Figure 3-2 illustrates, more than three-fourths of the respondents are executives. The companies that they work for include research institutions, services firms, financial services firms, software companies, manufacturing companies, telecommunications companies, consulting firms, computer companies, and healthcare organizations. Despite what you may think, the

Figure 3-3. Top operational problems survey—what respondents said.

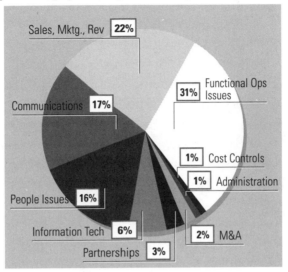

*Only 1% indentified controlling costs as
one of their top two operational concerns.
Total is less than 100 percent due to rounding*

answers do not consistently track with the kind of company involved. The specific issues vary, but the overall categories of issues (see Figure 3-3) don't. Functional and revenue issues are just as important in healthcare as they are in financial services as they are in software. Statistically, cost control is not important in any industry.

Day-to-Day Functional Issues

A third of the answers relate to the day-to-day running of the department or function and are focused internally to the business. As you look beyond that, the functional issues differ a great deal. A manager of business development for a software services company lists a concern for "understanding the state of various projects that need immediate communication and nurturing; prioritizing these correctly for short-term and long-term business development." A vice president with an international telecommunications company notes the problem of "management of real-time business information [concerning] sales, customers, and business metrics." For this VP, the issue is not information technology but the information itself. The director of operations for an international consulting firm identifies "monitoring for compliance with the operating policies and procedures of the company" as a top concern. The managing director of a venture capital company describes "taking new, relatively complex processes and developing systems [both IT and non-IT] so that personnel farther down on the chain of command can manage them effectively."

Processes appear in the executives' list often. A sales vice president at a software company says simply that a key issue is "process improvement. . . . Are we making it easy to do business with [the company]?" The general manager of a financial services business worries about "identifying and defining complete implementation procedures . . . to reduce client impact during new product introduction."

Infrastructure problems are also common. Several executives note how much difficulty they have getting basic services, and they seem frustrated. Making tools work (i.e., the tool's usefulness) garners the largest number of exclamation points among all the answers. This issue of usefulness goes beyond computers; it includes e-mail, phones, lights, offices, and buildings. The general manager of a communications division of a large vendor vents that it was "difficult to show others [meeting with me] in my office . . . the data on my computer screen, and too much of my desk is occupied with communications devices, like the conference phone, wireless phone, desktop phone."

Sales, Marketing, and Revenue Issues

Almost a quarter of the survey responses focus on the external view, or problems that deal with making deals happen, marketing to groups of customers, product marketing, and ensuring that the committed revenue streams actually arrive. Again, at this level of detail no operational problems cover every company. The survey results also show that title and position do not determine answers.

One software CEO says that his company "is currently rebranding, repositioning itself." The challenges include "balancing a transition from old to new without disturbing/impacting revenue." The CEO of a software services company highlights "forging our value proposition into our client communications and marketing message." The head of a consulting firm is struggling with "how to overcome the clients' resistance created by the 'newness' of the service."

Instead of a focus on how to manage individual products or services, product management reflects in the answers as a broader strategy issue. The chief technology officer (CTO) from an international software company wants to "formulate the midterm product roadmap." The CEO of a network products company is concerned with "expanding the product portfolio to cover additional markets."

As you might expect, new markets ranked high. The CEO of a hot network products company worries about "growing the company's ability to compete in markets beyond the obvious extensions of the [original] market." The CEO of a European software firm's U.S. division focuses on "identifying new market niches to exploit." The vice president of sales for an international telecommunications firm simply answers that the key issue is "development of new markets."

Lessons from the Operational Issues Survey

You can take some lessons from this research. First, all the problems are complicated. They will not be dealt with by easy or common solutions. Your best and most creative people need a great deal of ingenuity to solve these issues.

Additionally, none of these problems is easily addressed by a software package or a single product. If you want to deal with these problems, you must find a different kind of offering.

A corollary to this point is the fact that you cannot get the level of problem detail you want from an electronic survey. At best, you can see a general trend of where not to go, but not enough to know where to go. Chapter 4 will show you a better tool—the informational interview. The informational interview will cost you more time, people, and money, but the results will be much more valuable.

Perhaps most important, one message is clear: If you wish to deal with the most important problems facing this audience of executives, you will not want to focus on saving money. Almost none of the problems cited by the executives are solved by cost control. Saving money always matters, but compared with day-to-day operational issues and revenue issues, it pales. While most business-to-business sales presentations highlight cost savings, only one executive identified that as one of her top two concerns. If you focus on cost savings, you are missing the target and making it harder to create your new market. If you focus your new market on a cost-savings plan for your customers, it may work. If you focus it on increasing revenue, you have a much better chance of success.

Sophistication Versus Success

The more important the problem or worry is, the more value results from providing a solution. That value can be expressed as easier access to critical resources, increased revenue, and/or increased margins. The solution need not appear elegant or sophisticated. If technical polish were required, Palm and America Online would not be market dominators. Their lesson to us is that they have succeeded by hiding great technical and operational skills behind a simple view for the user. What we want in new markets is to build a combination of products and services that has the highest possible value to the prospective customer, not to us. A key to your success is to focus on the problem to be solved before you focus on the solution.

4

Choosing the Best Risk

Solving problems is not risk free. Knowing that you want to solve a problem leaves you with the challenge of deciding which problem to solve. This challenge will make a key difference to your decision of how to approach new market creation. If you choose the wrong problem to solve, you may cripple your chances of success.

To choose the right problem, you have three fundamental options (see Figure 4-1). You can try to:

►Anticipate future problems.

►Create problems that you can then resolve with your products.

►Go ask customers directly about their existing problems.

Which approach is most likely to bring you success in creating and dominating new markets? You may choose to use one, two,

Note: Portions of this chapter originally appeared in *Getting Started in Computer Consulting*, by Peter Meyer (New York: John Wiley & Sons, 2000), Chapter 5, "Marketing and Selling Your Services." Reprinted by permission of John Wiley & Sons, Inc.

Figure 4-1. Three overlapping options to find and choose the correct problem to solve.

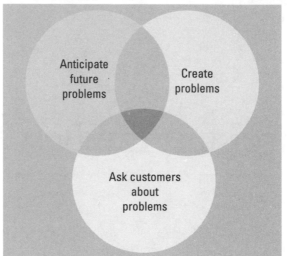

or all three methods. However, one of these approaches will consistently do better than the other two. Let's explore that.

Anticipating Problems

The most common decision is to anticipate problems—to look into the future and identify the most likely issues that will block the success of your customers. This strategy is attractive because, as the expert in your area, you probably know more about likely problems than 99 percent of the customers with whom you deal.

If you know how data and voice networks operate, you can identify the likely security risks from current designs. As you look at future designs, you can identify the most likely risks as well. If Microsoft implements scripting in the Outlook product, you may see that it creates three specific vulnerabilities in the product, or that corporate users are likely to generate a specific set of exposures. Anticipating these hazards can allow you to create a set of products that might sell quite well.

This strategy has worked well for several new markets. More often, however, the strategy fails. Many companies predicted a gas supply crisis in the 1990s, and some built products to help solve it. Several manufacturers produced and shipped electric and hybrid electric/gasoline cars, but the problem did not materialize. In fact, the reverse happened in the western United States when several states started to run out of electric power generating capacity.

Predicting a problem, Chrysler gambled six years and half its emergency cash infusion on the minivan concept in the 1970s. In 1977, Chrysler started initial development of a product that would fill the space between a full-size van and a station wagon. The automaker felt that it could create a market based on a new vehicle idea: a comfortable van that would fit in garages. According to Ralph Sarotte, general product manager for the minivan platform at DaimlerChrysler AG, "Large vans couldn't fit into people's garages. We knew if we could manufacture a fuel-efficient van that could fit into a garage and retain the walk-through feature of a van, we could very well be on our way to inventing a new segment in the automobile industry."[1]

The risk was substantial. It would take six years to launch the product set. The company could not afford the investment until the federal Chrysler Loan Guarantee Board approved $1.5 billion in guaranteed loans. Of that, the company spent almost half to create the market that is now minivans. This was, to a great extent, a decision to bet the company.

Although Chrysler did substantial market research, it did not know what problem it was solving. It discovered that most owners wanted to see where the front end of the car was, so the automaker mounted a Chrysler emblem where the hood ended. However, consumers did not find a compelling reason to buy the product. This made the minivan a high-risk proposition.

For Chrysler, the risk paid off. The market quickly grew, and the company reports sales of more than 9 million minivans. The volumes continue to increase, with sales of 1.6 million minivans in the year 2000. In that year, Chrysler had a 40 percent market share, continuing to dominate the market that the company helped to create. For this company, in this instance, anticipating and meeting its customers' needs worked.

It did not work for the Edsel or the DeLorean, cars that were introduced by the Ford Motor Company and the DeLorean Motor Company, respectively. Each failed to gain enough sales to sustain the business. Nor did it work for thousands of other products created in anticipation of a growing need. Two examples (as introduced in Chapter 3) are online grocery services and ISDN.

Webvan's management anticipated a problem that's been predicted often—a decreasing quality of life among families. With the increasingly hectic pace of modern life in the United States, the problem assumes, consumers have less disposable time than ever. Therefore, quality of life is worth even more than before. To get it, people will pay a premium (measured in hours invested) to get more time with their family or even with their television. If this becomes true, consumers will change their habits and plan grocery lists in advance if they can get additional disposable time. Webvan's plan was to make it easy for shoppers to save time by having groceries delivered to their home. The market? Every grocery shopper in every major city. Drivers for growth? As the pace of life increased, more shoppers would come to Webvan to save hours per week.

It didn't work that way. That long-anticipated problem did not unfold quickly enough to save the company.

The same thing occurred with Integrated Services Digital Network (ISDN) products. The anticipated problem was a growing need for high-speed (i.e., 64 Kbps to 128 Kbps) connectivity at homes and desks. Using ISDN products, a home or business owner could get the higher speeds without having to have additional phone lines installed. Telephone companies could deliver the speeds over old copper wires, avoiding the costs (in time, people, and money) of tearing up streets and communities. As the need for faster connections would grow, the products would sell well. It didn't happen. The desire for speed to the desktop was real, but not intensely enough to manifest support for a new market.

Anticipating problems is easy. Anticipating the problem that eventually becomes real enough to build a market is much riskier.

Creating Problems

A less popular but still successful path is to create problems. Where you know that you can create a serious problem, and then solve it, you have the opportunity to engender a new market. When you control the problem, controlling the market is easier. To do this can be as simple as taking features away from a product or service.

In California, Pacific Bell used to service the wiring from your phone all the way to the central office. If you had a problem, you would simply call the telephone company and complain. They would dispatch a technician. You would get a repair at no additional cost.

In the 1980s, as AT&T was breaking up for the first time, Pacific Bell changed this policy. The company no longer offers free service for wiring inside your home. If you have a problem, service technicians will come to your home and look at where that problem might be. If it is between your home and their central office, they take responsibility at no cost, just as before. However, if they diagnose your problem to be between the point where your line enters the house and your phone, the responsibility is yours. Of course, Pacific Bell will repair it for you if you ask, but they now charge you for that service. By withdrawing service, Pacific Bell created a new market for fee-based home repair services.

The company then offered a solution. For a small fee per month, it would offer you the same level of service that you had earlier. The service that you get has not improved substantially, if at all. However, the cost to get the service has become a revenue opportunity for telephone companies. The market for fixing telephone wire problems is significant in size.

Most homeowners view Pacific Bell as the logical vendor for that service, and the utility has dominated the market ever since. Now the company has a new market and income that comes from the decision to provide the same service that the utility withdrew earlier. Pacific Bell created the opportunity by creating a problem, and then stepped in to fix that problem.

Inkjet printer cartridges and razor blades offer a similar story. Getting the initial service and function is cheap and easy. You can get a razor for a few dollars, and inkjet printers are now available for $100. The idea? Hook you on the service; then, to continue to get the value you want from it, you have to buy products from the manufacturer that will cost you much more than the razor or printer.

Neither problem is earth-shattering to most users. People who own printers simply want to print photographs or documents. It's the same case that Apple Computer made for desktop publishing in the 1980s and 1990s. To have complete control over what you want to create and to be able to create it on your own schedule, you need to own the tools. Inkjet printers are a key tool for presenting the image that the user wants to project, whether it's letterhead or calling cards for business purposes or other graphics and documents for home use.

Vendor promotion strategies for inkjet printers are primarily focused on helping consumers feel the problem and buy ink. This represents a change in strategy. When printers were first introduced, ink was inexpensive. Suppliers kept the price of ink low to increase the number of printers sold. However, like razors, printers are not a frequent purchase. Ink is. If the printer companies (e.g., Hewlett-Packard, Canon, Epson, Brother, Lexmark) can make it more and more desirable to want desktop color printing, they can sell more ink.

The issue, then, is keeping control of ink sales. It would be of no use to Hewlett-Packard and the others if you could cheaply and easily buy ink from other suppliers. To complete the market opportunity, the printer companies have strategies to capture the ink business. Using product design, patents, attorneys, warranties, and market pressure, the printer suppliers have made it difficult for users to buy other brands of ink. The profit margin for printer ink is very high; it more than makes up for the low margins on the printers themselves. To a great extent, creating the problem is a marketing issue. It is to the advantage of the printer suppliers to make sure that you can buy only from them. The profit in the problem of not being able to print is large.

Printer companies, like the razor blade companies before them, have created a new market by creating a problem. This strategy brings several important risks. One is that you may create a competitor. If the cost of entering your market is low, another company can produce a similar product at a low cost. The raw materials that you buy are one cost. The cost of protecting the market is another. You may find that you have to spend more money on attorneys than you do on raw materials. Making and selling ink is relatively easy for others, so Hewlett-Packard and the other suppliers have to invest a great deal of time, people, and money in protecting their patents.

Another risk is that your customers may not be willing to

accept your answer. If you force them to pay more, they may just refuse. Some printer owners will switch to laser printing (which requires different and lower-cost consumables). Some trade magazines have started to rank printers by the annual cost of ink as well as by print quality. *PC Magazine* noted that "costs (per page) range from seven to twenty-eight cents per page, with the median average at eleven cents. When we calculated the three-year cost of ownership (ink plus printer cost), the most expensive printer . . . actually proved cheaper to own than three $100 to $150 printers." By the magazine's calculations, a $70 Lexmark printer would cost $2,511 to own and feed over a three-year period. A $900 Hewlett-Packard inkjet printer would cost almost $1,000 less by the time you factor in cost to buy ink over the three-year life of the product.[2]

You might expect high-consumption printers to be a dying product. You might want to change your strategy to focus on low-consumption printers. Losing revenue to sales of lower-cost consumables (such as cheaper ink or razor blades) seems to be a substantial risk. However, that is not usually the case. Managers and owners are often surprised at just how elastic pricing can be. Consumers have learned to pay much more for ink in the past decade, and inkjet printing has still increased significantly.

Airline costs were high enough, so it was said in the early 1990s, that business air travel would drop if prices increased again. You can see just how much elasticity exists in air travel pricing by looking at the numbers:

	Typical Business Fare	*Business Revenue Miles*
1993	$346	195 billion
2000	$539	276 billion
Increase	56 percent	42 percent

Sources: U.S. Department of Transportation, American Express, and United Airlines.

In 1993, U.S. airlines flew about 195 billion revenue passenger miles for business. Since then, many businesses have perceived that the cost increased substantially and service worsened at the same time.

The perception about prices was correct. In that period, the typical business fare rose from $346 to $539, an increase of 56 percent. You might expect that worse service at a higher price might result in fewer miles flown. Instead, in the year 2000, the number of business revenue passenger miles increased to about 276 billion miles.[3] That is an increase of 42 percent in miles flown and paid for. Customers grumbled, but paid the price to get to business meetings. The price of air travel in the 1990s was not as big a problem as the needs that drove business travel. Cost was secondary.

Hooking consumers and businesses on products is a function of finding the right problem to solve. With the right problem, price becomes much less of an issue than your ability to deliver a solution.

The issue is creating the right problem. If you create a wonderfully important problem, you can name your price. However, most "created" problems do not work that well.

Creating problems is risky, expensive, and not always successful. The consumer and business products that fail each year far outnumber the ones that succeed. If you want to reduce that risk, consider finding a problem instead of creating it.

Asking About Problems

Asking is hard for many managers and owners. You might assume that customers expect us to anticipate problems. You may not feel comfortable questioning prospective customers out of concerns about bothering them. Sometimes, you may not want to hear any answer but the one that is most comfortable for you. Nonetheless, if you want to know where you have the best chance of creating a new market, the key may be in simply asking about the problems that your prospective customers would pay the most to solve.

These are not the same as the problems that your customers would consider to be the most pervasive. In Chapter 1, we looked at the temptation to build the proverbial better mousetrap. You may be able to build one, and some major cities in the developing world have a massively pervasive problem with rats. However, they don't see a need to control the problem. Although they have rats, they aren't willing to pay to remove them.

Key to creating a lasting market is asking the right question. If the question is, "What is the right problem to solve?" then you must ask that question of the people whom you want to become customers. If prospective customers consistently tell you that a specific problem is real and at the top of their list, you have a natural area to focus your products and services.

Beyond the concerns many managers and owners express about talking to customers, there are two fundamental risks:

▶You may not know what to ask.

▶You may not like the answer.

Knowing what to ask is not difficult. The informational interview process in the next section can guide you through the questions. The principle is straightforward—to get the answer, simply go to people who might be future customers and ask: "What keeps you up at night?"

Then listen. Be careful not to sell to your interviewees. Instead, let them sell you on their problems. You are looking for information now so that you can create a market in the near term. The informational interview is designed to give you bits of information. If you ask fifty potential customers, you will see a trend. That trend will tell you which problems your customers will pay to solve.

Of course, it's possible that you may not like the trend when you find it. You may have invested too much time, too many people, too much money, or even too much of yourself in a different problem.

The answers you get will not be the right problem to solve, but they will reflect the symptoms as the customers see them. However, these answers can lead you to a good problem. For instance, your prospective customers may tell you that they need a new sales channel, but the answer may be for you to use automated tools to improve the existing channels. Your team of managers from marketing, sales, and finance will bring the knowledge and skill to extrapolate to the right problem. However, that only works if you extrapolate *from* the right problem. That starts with a good informational interview.

Informational Interviews

Just as in diagnosing a technical problem, the key to getting to the right business problem is to ask the right questions. One process for this is the informational interview model. In this model, you find your target prospective clients and ask them questions. The informational interview model has six steps that, taken together, define a roadmap for examining a business market.

The informational interview is built on six principles that reinforce the six steps shown in Figure 4-2 in the process and are the keys to making the process work:

Principles of an Informational Interview Process

1. Look for people whom you would normally not approach, as well as people whom you would.

2. No selling is allowed. These are not customers; they are information sources you value.

3. Ask few questions, and none about products. Ask only about problems.

4. Do not offer solutions, no matter how tempted you are.

5. Listen more, talk less. Bury your ego.

6. If you do not have time to do the interview right, hire someone who can.

Figure 4-2. Roadmap to informational interviews.

1	Choose the managers whose problems matter the most to you.
2	Call the managers, asking for information to create a new market (not to sell).
3	Structure two questions that will find the top problems from the manager's perspective.
4	Ask the questions, and do much more listening than talking. Do not solve problems.
5	Add more managers to the process, get more perspectives.
6	As applicable, return to key managers to offer solutions or get more information.

Chapter 7 gives details on the Gauss case that is based on this model. For now, let's explain the six-step process in general terms.

Step 1: Whom Will You Talk To?

The first step is to identify whom you will target for a new market. When you choose to create a new market, your best bet is to start with a potential customer set that you want to attract. Most likely, these potential customers do not know that they might become a market.

If you are interested in creating a new market among known customers (see Chapter 5), you have an obvious place to start. Of course, you may not want to limit yourself to that audience. It may be useful to spread out to different potential customers. This spread would be both across different companies and markets and different positions. A common mistake in surveying customers is to work only with your existing customers. Your answers will be much more useful if you reach out to customers who have chosen *not* to buy from you in the past. Unless you are especially dominant in the existing market, you have more noncustomers than customers for your product. Chances are that they have more to tell you as well.

If you are interested in customer sets that you do not know, you will have to make educated guesses. This may mean more interviews, but better results. In the Gauss case (discussed in Chapter 7), the net was cast very wide and the information attained was very valuable.

If you are thinking of creating a new software application for existing customers and you want to enter the banking market in your community, you can go to several different people, such as the bank's data center operations manager, the information systems (IS) executive, or the end-users. Depending on the bank, one or another of these groups may have more authority when it comes to discussing software applications. A smart decision is to talk to all three.

The same is true if you want to go after just one account. You may have four or five different end-user communities from which to choose. Sales will have different requirements than engineering. Marketing will have another need, and finance will be looking for something entirely different. If in doubt, talk to senior managers in each area. It cannot hurt to start wide and then narrow your list of managers as you proceed. Always interview people whom you think (or know) would not buy from your business.

Interviewing should be done in person and by staff members who will listen well and talk less. What you are looking for is a problem description as the customer sees the issue, not as someone else might define it. That means getting a live conversation is critical. Web interviews, written questionnaires, and automated processes will not gather the information that you need. You have the option of:

▶Asking the questions yourself

▶Having your team ask the questions

▶Having a specialty firm conduct the interview

There are few such specialty firms (one is described in the Gauss example in Chapter 7) that will put call quality ahead of call volume considerations. When you choose such a firm, be sure to get references that will attest to the quality of the listening skills of the callers. No matter which of the three options you choose for conducting the informational interview, remember that only phone or personal interviews will get you the essential problem information that you need.

At this point, you are not calling on customers or potential customers. You are calling on people who can help define a market. If you consider them customers, you may find yourself "selling" to them instead of doing an informational interview. The purpose of this project is to get information, not give it. Effectively, you are buying, not selling. As much as possible, consider these contacts to be managers instead of customers. Choose the managers who can give you the most difficult and important problems to solve.

Step 2: Calling Managers

In step 2, you need to drop the self-focus entirely and adopt a customer focus. It matters little what your business wants or can do. What matters is what the managers from the company want and feel. Your ego has to recede into the background.

To do step 2, call each manager and ask for an informational interview. In this request make three points clear:

1. The interview is informational only. You are looking to work in this community/market/industry/company and you want the perspective of this particular manager before you decide to start.

2. You are looking for the answers to two specific questions. You will not ask vague questions. You are focused on specific information.

3. When you have answers from all of your research, you will be pleased to share it (without names) with any of the managers who were kind enough to help.

Once you have an appointment, prepare only one or two key questions that will elicit the problem information that you want to get.

Step 3: Structuring Your Two Questions

A basic tenet of markets is that the more desirable the customer, the busier that person is. That means the prospective customer has little time to invest in being sold something that is not on the top of that manager's list of worries.

A corollary is that these same managers are smart enough to want to meet the best people whenever they can. Who are the best people? They are:

▶Quick thinkers with good judgment

▶Bright enough to look for background information

▶Focused in what they ask for

▶Willing to collect a variety of viewpoints before they make a decision

The best people rarely proclaim themselves. They show their strengths by asking good questions. The questions that you ask will likewise build the image of your business.

With that in mind, it makes sense to go into the interview with several questions, but only ask two. Avoid wasting your time on questions related to product or technical issues. Instead, focus on business issues. Here is a list of questions that you may want to start with:

Sample Questions to Open Informational Interviews

▶What keeps you up at night?

▶Why *should* your customers buy from you? Why *do* they buy from you?

▶Why do you lose customers?

▶Where is the next market that this company wants to enter? What is slowing down the company's entry into that market?

▶If you could wave a wand to solve any problem that you wish, which problem would it be?

These questions put the focus where it belongs—on the manager and the business instead of on you. It also allows you to learn more about the business than you would find out by asking about products or services. This focus signals to the manager that you are not just interested in technical issues, you care about the business and about the issues that matter to the manager.

If you call twenty people, you may only get ten informational interviews. If a person you really want to talk to is unavailable, keep going down the list. You can go back to them during step 5. First, talk to the ten managers in an informal setting.

Step 4: Coffee and the Interview

The fourth step is to hold the informational interviews. In an ideal world, you would sit down informally over a cup of coffee with a manager. As you chat, take notes, ask follow-up questions for clarification, but observe these three key rules:

1. No selling allowed. No matter what the manager says, you are here to ask and not tell.

2. Avoid offering solutions. You may pick up on something so obvious that you are dying to impress the manager by stating it. Instead, ask if that solution is important. If the answer is yes, say you may know an answer. Ask for permission to call back with the right solution. Don't offer it at this conversation.

3. Focus completely on the manager. Bury your ego.

Many interviews work well with only one question: "I want to know more about your business. Can you tell me what keeps you up at night?" The result is exactly what you want—a discussion of what really matters to the manager and the business.

When you are done, thank the manager and offer to share a summary of what you find from all of your conversations. Most managers will be interested. If you think you can help the manager, suggest that you want to think about the problem and will call back with an idea when you are sure it will work. Do not supply an answer in the interview.

As you do the interviews, watch for interesting trends and responses. Try to identify the drivers that help the business run, and study the problems about which you have heard. If some global solutions come to you, note them for yourself and for step 6. If the information warrants it, write up the responses as a short report or presentation. Remember to keep individual responses confidential.

Step 5: Whom Else Should You Contact?

The penultimate step is to look at the list of contacts you have left on your list and go back to some of them. For every ten managers you ask for an interview, some will say no and some won't respond. You may still want to talk to them. In addition, you may have collected some more names as you proceeded. Many managers to whom you talked in step 4 may suggest other names to call.

Some people on your still-want-to-talk-to-them list will be strangers that others have referred to you. Some will be managers that you have previously identified but were not available to you originally. Some of these people will be managers whom you chose not to work with but were advised to contact.

In any of these cases, call the individual and say something like the following: "I have talked to [name some influential managers] and several recommended you. Before I make any final decisions, I'd like to get the benefit of your input. Can I get a few minutes with you to ask two specific questions?" If you can drop someone's name, and also if you emphasize the word *final*, that will often be enough to get you some more interviews.

When all these interviews are done and you understand the problems, it is time to consider which ones you want to solve. Only after you know which ones you want to solve should you look at how to solve them. With that information, you can go back to the key managers with whom you want to work over time.

Step 6: Start Solving Problems

Your final step is to go back to the managers with whom you would like to develop a vendor/customer relationship. Suggest that you think you understand the problem and have a solution that may help them. This may be the perfect way to move into the product development cycle with friendly testers.

If you promised a summary of the findings, remember to send it. You may get some very interesting responses. Some of those responses may make a difference in how you approach the problems and how you create the new market.

Are You Too Far Invested in the Wrong Problem?

As we have seen, many companies provide solutions that they find attractive for internal reasons, but are not all that attractive to customers. These companies create new products that solve problems that customers don't value highly.

If the customer thinks that your problem is less important than his or her problem, you will have a hard time getting mind share.

When that happens, you have two solutions between which you can choose. The first is to try to make your problem feel more important. For this solution, a great sales and marketing team is essential. You make the problem that you want to solve seem so overwhelming that the customer has no real choice but to come to you. Escalating the criticality of a problem is a great short-term solution.

The longer-term solution is to be willing to leave a problem behind. No matter how much you have invested in the problem, investing any more of your resources may be pouring good money after bad. You cannot spend your way out of the fact that you are solving the wrong problem; you can only leave your investment behind.

In 1984, Federal Express tried to create and dominate a second market—instant document delivery. The company had already created and still dominated the overnight-delivery market. That gave it offices and delivery people in every major city in the United States. By setting facsimile transmission systems in offices across the country, the company hoped to allow businesses to send documents electronically for same-day delivery. It was an interesting idea that would take advantage of the Federal Express delivery staff that already dropped off the morning packages. The company called the service ZapMail and launched the service nationwide.

The problem was that the same facsimile technology that FedEx bought soon became available to its customers, at a very low cost. If a business could buy a fax machine for $300, it did not make sense to pay another company a fee to collect, transmit, and then hand-deliver the same fax.

FedEx pursued the idea, finally investing thousands of person-hours, five years, and more than $300 million to solve a problem that customers did not rate highly. If the management of the company had been willing to walk away from their investment early, they would have avoided much of that loss.[4]

The same management team did not walk away from its investment to create the overnight-delivery service. That was a wise, if difficult, decision. What was the difference between the core service in the early days and the ZapMail service? The primary difference was that the problem of overnight delivery of packages was real and no one else was solving it. ZapMail did not solve any real problem.

You owe it to yourself to be critical in your analysis of problems. When you find that you have invested in the wrong problem, leave it behind. If you want to create and dominate a new market, choose to invest in and solve the most critical problem.

Problems Fade—So Does Market Domination

Even as you choose the dominant problem, your success can become a source of failure. If you solve the problem completely, you will be out of a market.

The good news is that this is rarely the case. More frequently you will find that you have a long list of people or businesses that perceive that the problem is real. As you work down that list, solving the problem, you work to satisfy the first customers with additional offerings and then go on to the next customers. You may never run out of customers.

However, you may find yourself short of customers who are economically feasible for you. Dominating a local market for healthcare services is a function of marketing to patients and doctors. Moving to a remote market two counties away is more expensive in terms of time, people, and money. Moving to another state or time zone is much more expensive as well. The market may be available, but you may not want to go after it.

A deeper concern is that problems change in severity. Building a better buggy whip is not as important now as it was 150 years ago. Electronic data interchange (EDI) solutions are not as important this decade as they were twenty years ago. If you develop a wonderful EDI solution tomorrow, you may not have much success. The right problem to solve will be a moving target.

Sometimes a problem returns, and faith is rewarded. If you made solar energy products in the 1970s, you may have done well. In the 1980s and 1990s, you may have stayed in business hoping for a resurgence. In 2001, you would have gotten that resurgence in the western United States. You would have been rewarded for staying the course.

The problem is knowing whether you are on the buggy whip path or the solar energy path. One way to find out is to wait. Another is to return to what works, then go to your potential customers and ask them what keeps them up at night. Many managers assume that once they have built a success in a market, they know where it will go. That tendency to hubris is the tendency to fading market domination.

5

What New Markets Are Available to You?

Creating and dominating a new market is always a difficult task, but you can make it easier if you work systematically. You can follow four paths to create a new market, some of which are easier than the others. You have the option of consciously choosing one or another of the paths, and that deliberate choice can eliminate a number of tangents for your team and increase your chances of success. Which of the four paths you choose will always depend on the circumstances of your business.

As you look at markets, your choices are that you can attempt to create a new market:

▶With unknown products and unknown customers

▶With a known product and unknown customers

▶With an unknown product and known customers

▶With known products and customers

Figure 5-1 shows how these four market definitions relate. It also shows that creating and dominating new markets is easier

Figure 5-1. New markets are new customers and/or new products.

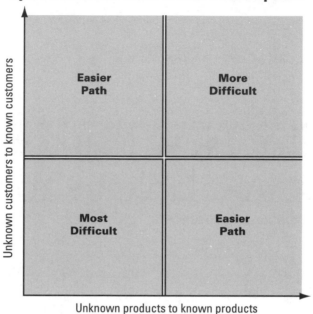

*Creating and dominating new markets is easier when you
start with either products or customers that you know, but not both.*

when you start with either products or customers that you
know, but not both.

The most difficult path is highlighted in Figure 5-2: unknown products and unknown customers. Following that route,
you have no real-world knowledge of potential customers or
products. The risk of failure is higher; the work to avoid that
failure is more difficult.

If you have knowledge of either your products or your potential customers, you can reduce uncertainty. Your experience
will cut the time and effort required to shrink risk even further.
Working from the upper left or lower right quadrants is working
from a position of greater strength.

Perhaps counterintuitively, when you move to the upper

Figure 5-2. Unknown products and unknown customers are the most difficult path to creating new markets.

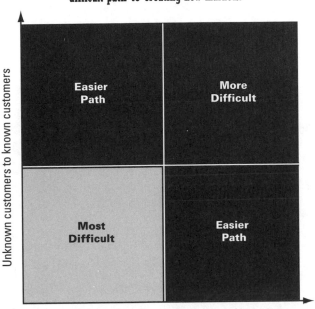

Unknown products to known products

right quadrant and acquire a knowledge of both products *and* customers you find that your task gets more difficult again. Having both makes it more likely that your existing markets will define you. Knowing your products and customers well tends to lead to line extensions instead of new products. There is nothing wrong with this position, but it does not create and dominate new markets. Working in the upper right quadrant makes it likely that you will rely too much on your experience.

Path 1: New Customers, New Products

For many executives, the most exciting prospect is to go after new customers and new products together. Starting from the equivalent of a blank slate allows the most creativity, and that can be fun.

When you do not know your prospective customers well, you have the challenge of learning about them. You may be able to define the customers and their expectations as you go, showing them the traits that define their future needs and problems. Then you can possibly dictate the solutions that they should use to solve those problems.

The same excitement can come from being able to create new products. You can decide what the product should do, how it should look, and how it should go about resolving the problem that you defined. Creating a product from scratch can be immensely satisfying. The only problem is that there may not be a business opportunity.

One example of a company that pursued new products and customers is Mosaic/Netscape Communications. Today you may look at the company as a failed effort. Netscape is no longer the most popular World Wide Web (WWW) browser and the company does not exist except as a brand name inside America Online. However, when Netscape started (as Mosaic), it was one of two companies that hoped to take advantage of the Mosaic web browser developed at the University of Illinois.

The Mosaic Communications team hoped to create and then dominate the market for web browsers. Their plan was to use the Mosaic browser, a known product, to help create a market of unknown customers. To succeed, Mosaic would have to accomplish two tasks. First, the company would have to convert millions of users who never saw a need for a browser. Most of the users did not even know what the World Wide Web was, much less why they cared and would want to take the trouble to install and use a browser.

The second objective Mosaic had to realize was to start over with a new product. The company faced a serious legal problem.

Although Mosaic Communications employed some of the software's authors and architects, it did not have the rights to the software or even the name Mosaic. Spyglass, Inc. had worked with the university to acquire those rights. When Marc Andreessen and Jim Clark formed Mosaic Communications in April 1994, Spyglass had been in business for almost four years and already had a relationship with the University of Illinois. By August 1994, Spyglass owned the rights to Mosaic software. Since Spyglass had the same general goals as Mosaic Communications, the older company was not willing to share the rights to use the name and product. To succeed, Mosaic Communications had to abandon the Mosaic product, the company's name, and then build a browser from scratch.

In October, Mosaic Communications released the beta version of the Netscape product. As a new browser, it was not yet complete. However, it was enough of a product for the company to have an offering. A month later, the company changed its name to Netscape Communications, and in December 1994 the newly named company reached an agreement with the University of Illinois that allowed Netscape to go forward without interference. The company did go forward, creating a new market and then dominating it for years until Microsoft Corp. wrested that dominance away.

In many ways, the success of Netscape was totally improbable. The team had created a new product that had no history or experience. They had targeted a group of prospective customers who did not know why they might want the product. To make the market work, Netscape had to give away the new product. Even this step was difficult. Netscape didn't yet know whom to target for giving away the product!

The company's core assumption was that the World Wide Web would be so attractive that people would invest time in learning how to use it. Once they discovered the Web, the assumption continued, companies would want to market ideas (i.e., advertising) and products (i.e., e-commerce) to those people. The Netscape browser would be the tool to help customers self-select, and the commercial companies would spend money to buy the software that would talk to these individual users. Netscape would give the user "client" software away, but sell the "server" products to the commercial companies. This idea worked and Netscape became a going concern dominating a new market.

Many other companies have tried a similar path, creating a new and free technology product for new customers. However, some made the critical mistake of attacking a problem that didn't need a solution. Attractive technology and no dollar cost are not enough. Installation and support are not free. Each of these products carries a substantial time cost for consumers, and often a time and people cost for businesses. The result of providing a solution that has no problem is predictable. In 2000, a number of websites popped up with the sole intention of tracking failed dot-com companies—Failuremag.com, Dotcomfailures. com, Startupfailures.com, and Sandhilltoad.com, to name a few. Upside magazine also kept a list of failures, some well known and some not known outside of a small group of friends. Ironically, several of these sites have gone under themselves.

One problem with having neither a known product nor a known customer is that you have a problem deciding which features to add or ignore. If you are solving a specific problem, you can add features that solve the problem as the customers see it. If you are not working a specific and well-defined problem, you may be building a product that will miss the mark.

The examples of attempts to create new markets by choosing path 1 are not all recent. 3M's Post-it Notes product line is an example of a success story. Electric cars in the 1990s are an example of a failure to create a market. In both cases the companies started with no clear idea of either the product or the prospective customers.

Building a product from scratch is hard enough. To define a customer set that never existed, and therefore may not know that they are potential customers, is a considerable effort. Doing both at once is exponentially difficult. The path of new products and new customers is the hardest strategy to follow, and the highest risk to your business.

Path 2: Unknown Products, Known Customers

The advantage of knowing your customers is that you can, with a reasonable investment in time and money, find out what problems matter to them the most. Then, as you develop your new products, you know what solutions you need to provide. Working with existing customers is a significant reduction in risk (see Figure 5-3).

Whereas Netscape had to find out who would be a potential customer, Frederick Smith built his first product plan for Federal Express on easily knowable customers: the Federal Reserve banks in the United States. As a customer set, these banks are easy to identify because there are a set number of them in locations that are well advertised. The reason that his initial plan to deliver their checks didn't work was not that the customer set was a mystery, but that Smith did not approach his prospective customers before he built his product plans to learn what he needed to know to get their business. Smith and his company learned from that experience and ultimately Federal Express identified a different set of known customers with whom to initiate the overnight package delivery market.

Edwin Land was a little more systematic about using a known set of customers. Although his idea came serendipitously

Figure 5-3. Unknown products and known customers are an easier path to creating new markets.

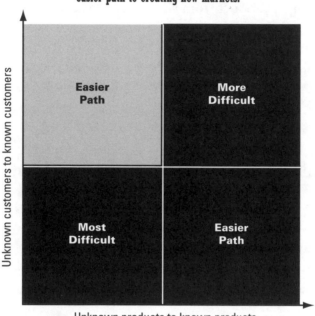

Unknown products to known products

(according to company lore, Land came up with the idea of a single-step photographic process after his daughter asked why she couldn't see the photograph right after he'd taken her picture), the inventor developed the instant camera product for a specific set of prospects. Land targeted hobbyist photographers, a small but known group of customers. With great success there, his company, Polaroid, moved into other consumer markets. Even so, throughout the first two decades of instant photography, Polaroid never ceased to dominate the professional and hobbyist market. A key marketing strategy was to use the endorsement of professional photographers such as Ansel Adams to build credibility. Simultaneously, the company used its patents to raise the barrier of entry for other companies. Land was able to create and then dominate a new market.

Not every story finishes with success. American Telephone and Telegraph (AT&T) created the Picturephone decades ago, with the intent of providing a visual phone call to every home. Although AT&T built the first units in 1956, the company did not test them with consumers until 1964.

As they started, the design team was working with a new product and known customers. AT&T, then a single national company, knew its customers better than anyone could ever hope to repeat. Nearly every home in the United States was in their records, and the company had near-perfect knowledge of the details of each phone renter. In 1964, the company could predict how many customers would buy Picturephone service and at what price point. The design team knew what they had to do to make the product attractive to these known customers. What the design team could not do was make the technology workable. Even today, the technology does not meet the needs defined back then.

The risk is always high with new technologies and unknown products. You may be able to identify a great set of customers who are ready to buy, but you still have to deliver. Polaroid did so; Federal Express eventually did so. AT&T's Picturephone group failed.

Path 3: Unknown Customers, Known Products

Another way to avoid the risk of new products is to find new markets for your existing products. Starting with existing products is not necessarily easier than using new products and known customers, but you will find it more likely to succeed than new products with new customers (see Figure 5-4). Many businesses have followed the new customers/known products path.

Figure 5-4. Known products and unknown customers are an easier path to creating new markets.

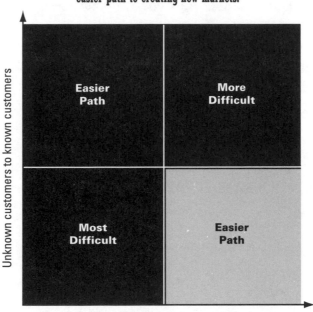

Unknown products to known products

During the 1980s and 1990s, analog cellular handsets were clearly becoming obsolete in the United States and Europe. As the market for analog cellular phones shrank, some companies built digital handsets and infrastructure while others did not. Moving to new handset technology is not an easy decision. To create a handset is expensive, and to base it on a technology (digital cellular) that was not yet accepted was risky. However, the risk did not stop there. The major cellular equipment providers either built or had tied themselves to a variety of infrastructure products that would also require a change. Conversion to a digital signal means conversion throughout the entire network. For digital handsets to work, a massive investment has to occur. New equipment must be placed on each cell tower. The vendor has to refresh the dealer network to handle the new product sets. New software has to be written and tested just to place calls and transfer them to and from the other parts of the network, or even other networks. Information technology and production teams must test and install new computers to run the new software. You can see why some companies that already knew and made analog cellular phones and infrastructures might want to find ways to leverage their existing expertise.

In the 1990s, while Nortel Networks built a new digital infrastructure and Nokia Corp. and Ericsson (among others) built new handsets, Motorola, Inc. went in a different direction. Motorola chose to take a known product to unknown customer sets in order to leverage its investment in known products, including the infrastructure.

Some of those new customer sets were in developing countries. This seemed a natural path considering that twenty years ago, many of these countries had billions of residents but no reasonable way for the national telephone utilities to provide wired service to homes. An inexpensive wireless network option was very attractive. Using wireless technology, the government-owned utilities could avoid the time and expense of installing a wire-based network. That is a considerable savings.

Such a conversion was not easy for Motorola or any other supplier. Different dial tones, technical specifications, power systems, and political issues made the provisioning of cellular service to other countries an ongoing operational challenge. Gaining the approval for a phone system in another country is a great deal of work. Creating a product and service distribution system is difficult. Providing technical support in other countries is difficult, too. Even so, these are known problems that will yield to an experienced and dedicated team.

Motorola's strategy, to use a known product with an unknown group of customers, was a way to speed the creation of new markets. The same strategy led to the adoption of AZT as a treatment for HIV disease. This drug had been developed to defeat cancer, but had failed in that application and was shelved. Almost by accident, doctors discovered this compound would temporarily stop AIDS from developing in a patient.

AZT was a known product, but details of the potential users of AIDS drugs were completely unknown in the 1980s. No one was entirely sure how HIV infected patients or how it survived in the human body for more than a decade without signs of infection. It took years to find the virus, and longer to find possible treatments for it. Before anyone identified AZT as a treatment, it appeared that any product would be very difficult to create or isolate. Even after AZT was adopted, more drugs would clearly be required. None of them were known and each would have to go through a difficult process to be brought to market.

On the customer side, it was unclear who the patients might be. Although the first patients were gay men, no one could project whether gay men were typical patients or simply the first group to be noticed. Medically, knowing the profiles of the patient community is important. From a market development perspective, no one could forecast what income levels customers would have, if they would be in a few cities or nationwide, or even how many customers there would be. The customer set was a complete mystery.

Choosing to use AZT, a known product with proven abilities to fight retroviruses such as HIV, considerably reduced the risk for the company that bought the rights to the drug, Burroughs Wellcome (which after a series of mergers is now GlaxoSmithKline PLC). The side effects had already been explored, and although they were severe, they were a known quantity. For this pharmaceutical, initial development was complete. This was important because it let the company focus on the market. Even with a known product, the customers presented many unanswered questions. For instance, no one knew which patients could tolerate the strong side effects of AZT. Most of the patients would have damaged immune systems, and it was not clear what would happen to those systems when AZT was introduced. As difficult as such unknowns are, however, the problems of understanding the customers can be solved with sufficient effort and dedication.

For some patients with HIV and AIDS, the new discovery was a near miracle. Word of the compound spread rapidly among patients and doctors, and the company brought it to market quickly in the 1980s, creating and dominating a new market for anti-retroviral drugs. AZT is still the "gold standard" by which new anti-retroviral drugs are measured, and GlaxoSmithKline has an enviable market share of anti-HIV drugs worldwide (40 percent) even now.[1]

Path 4: Known Customers, Known Products ✓

For most excellent operational managers, the most obvious strategy is to try to create a market from known customers and known products (see Figure 5-5). Intuitively, it seems that if you know both, you can probably reduce your risks commensurately. The problem in application comes in minimizing the risks too much and producing a line extension instead of a new market. Extending a line of products is very useful as a strategy to fund new market efforts, but line extensions are not new markets.

At my local supermarket, I can find six varieties of Tide brand detergent on the shelves, some offered in multiple sizes. The Tide website highlights seventeen separate products for the Canadian market. These come with bleach, without bleach, with

Figure 5-5. Known products and known customers are *not* an easier way to create new markets.

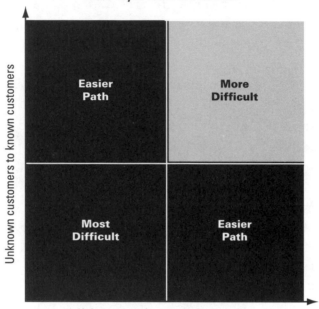

Unknown products to known products

bleach alternative, with and without special odor-reduction techniques, in Ultra and non-Ultra formulations, without dyes or perfumes, in liquid and powder and tablet varieties, and so on. Most of these come in different sizes, to allow for different needs and different buyers.

Each of these products is a line extension, a technique that takes an existing product family and widens it to be more appealing to other niches of users. Line extensions allow a good product manager to lengthen the life of a product and to find a little more revenue from customers who may otherwise buy a different product. For a market-dominating product, such as Tide brand detergent, product line extensions are a key strategy to retain that dominance. Good product management teams do this well. However, extending the dominance of a known product is different from creating and dominating a new market. For many management teams, the two concepts are contradictory. They see it as a question of resource and opportunity costs, and new markets cost too much.

In Chapter 2, Dr. Donald Francis, president of VaxGen, Inc., pointed out that his company could not exist inside a larger parent pharmaceutical company. For the larger companies, the knowledge of the treatments that sell and the customers who buy them makes it very easy to focus on past successes. In the pharmaceutical industry, the rate of product failure is already high. Companies can spend tens or hundreds of millions of dollars to develop a drug that fails to make it to stores and pharmacies. Developing treatments is a high-risk business. If you run a pharmaceutical company, you can save years and millions of dollars by simply working the known products and markets. New markets may seem like a luxury.

If you want to create a new market, it may be tempting to leverage your knowledge of products and customers as far as possible. By working the upper right-hand quadrant in Figure 5-6, you reduce your risk but also reduce the chance that you will build a new market. The risk to knowing your product and customers is that you will become defined by your knowledge. Being limited by experience is a benefit for line extensions but a liability for new markets. Relying on that knowledge can lead you into a competitive environment when you had hoped to wind up in a niche where you could dominate.

The Challenge

Despite some of the positive examples listed in Figure 5-6, failures far outnumber successes. The risk of failure in creating and

Figure 5-6. Examples of companies and their chosen paths to creating a new market.

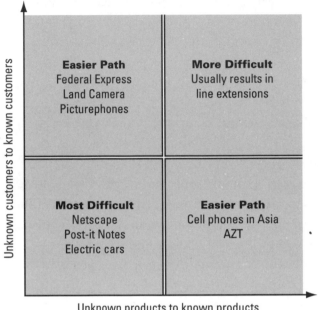

Easier Path
Federal Express
Land Camera
Picturephones

More Difficult
Usually results in
line extensions

Most Difficult
Netscape
Post-it Notes
Electric cars

Easier Path
Cell phones in Asia
AZT

Unknown customers to known customers

Unknown products to known products

*New markets can come via each of these paths, but
two of the paths are more likely to succeed.*

then dominating new markets is directly proportional to two seemingly contradictory factors:

1. Your lack of knowledge about the products and markets that you are addressing

2. The tendency to let yourself or your team be defined by the knowledge you do have

The solution to the first issue may be a management decision to leverage the knowledge that your team already has. If you know your product well, the path with a lower risk is to go find new customers. However, as your team explores these new customer sets you must remain open to changing the product to meet new needs. Remember that the product is not the technology. The product also includes the delivery process, all the customer interfaces for your company, support systems, accounting processes, and more. You may need to invest time, people, and money in making extensive changes. Adapting a phone system to a new country requires extensive changes in hardware, software, and support, for example. AZT as a compound did not need to be changed to dominate the new AIDS pharmaceutical market, but it required extensive testing, approvals, and marketing—all of which was incredibly expensive in terms of time, people, and money resources. And it was worth it.

As difficult as it may be to adapt and change a product that you know, not being bound by your previous knowledge can be harder still. You may find that the teams of managers and executives who excel at operational issues are not able to forget those issues and work on creating something new. You will need both mindsets, and that kind of mental fluidity is rare. Asking one person or team to handle both operational issues and new market creation usually results in a compromise where you are unable to do either job effectively. The best solution to the second issue may be to follow the path of IBM's PC team, Lockheed's Skunkworks, and countless business "incubators" and charter market creation teams that are separate from the rest of the company. Then, as the market is built, the market-creation team can take advantage of the operational excellence in the rest of your business.

When you overcome these challenges, you will number among the very small number of companies that are ready to attempt the creation of new markets. Your attempts may fail more often than they succeed, but the successes will be well worth the effort.

PART 2

Applications of the Strategies

6

Funding the New Market Effort

One challenge to creating and dominating new markets is the cost. You should not just measure this expense in cash, but also in terms of time and people. No matter how much or how little you have of those resources, every time you invest in a new market effort you are incurring an opportunity cost. The question becomes: How can you generate enough of those resources to subsidize a new market? Funding the new market effort is the subject of this chapter.

Many businesses pull focus, people, and money from existing work to feed growth and new markets. However, extracting resources from the existing business to feed the future carries two risks: It jeopardizes your existing business while you risk

Note: Parts of this chapter originally appeared in *Business Horizons* (November/December 1999) pp. 37–40, and are reprinted courtesy of the University of Indiana. Additional material in this chapter is adapted from "Finding the Funds for IT," *Business Communications Review* (March 1988), pp. 51–53, and from a presentation by the author at the Information Technology & Telecommunications Association (formerly the Tele-Communications Association) in 1998. Reprinted with permission.

the future on a speculative venture. If you do not have enough resources, both the existing business and the new market must do well simultaneously for either to survive. The question becomes: How can you get more money, people, and time from your existing operations to fund the new efforts? You can use many traditional techniques, but consider two newer ones as well—opportunity databases and dreams—that will give you more cash without going outside your business.

Opportunity Databases

One way to gain time, people, and money for new markets is to ask your organization to change how it focuses on prospective customers. Taking the time to create and use an opportunity database can help fund new efforts. The idea is simple. Make it easier for your sales teams and channels to call on the best prospects first.

Most sales teams and distributors call on prospects as demand-generation programs uncover them. Until recently, the best practices have relied on entreating prospects to respond using advertising, trade shows, direct mail, and seminars. The response is scattered and comes in without priority—only a few of the prospective clients react at any one time. With this process you can take the leads only as they come. Mediocre leads will get to the top of the list ahead of customers who should be the best leads. Your sales and your prospective customers both suffer when this happens.

There are better ways to fund your future. With the advent of faster computers, you can get more than just 25,000 prospective customers. With the advent of faster computers, you can ask and discover who each of the 25,000 are, their addresses, revenues, contacts, and buying patterns. With that information, your team can build an opportunity database that can sort most of your prospective customers at once and rank them by standards that you choose. It will have considerable effect on product development, pricing and margins, marketing, sales, and sales management. These effects help you get more resources for growth in existing or new markets.

Let's compare the results of traditional lead programs versus opportunity databases:

Traditional Lead Program	Opportunity Database
Looks at leads in a serial fashion	Looks at all leads at once
Finds prospects who feel need	Finds prospects before they feel need
Is limited to those people who respond	Looks at total universe of possible customers
Cost is very expensive per lead	Lower per-lead cost because main cost is up-front
Does not prioritize leads	Assigns rankings to all leads
Takes leads one by one	Provides macro, not micro, view
Is time- and people-intensive	Leverages technology
Does not rank leads by need (i.e., all leads are equal)	Ranks leads by likely sense of need
Mixes price-sensitive leads with others	Ranks leads by likely margin contribution

Freeing Resources for Growth

One positive aspect of looking at all your leads at once is that you can identify the prospective customers who have the most intense needs. These are the prospective customers who are (1) more likely to buy and (2) less price sensitive. When you know in advance which prospects are likely to pay more for your product you can reduce discounting and raise the average sales price. This incremental revenue drops directly to the bottom line, where it is available to fund new efforts. Figure 6-1 illustrates, in a simple way, this concept in which your sales team moves from the scattered incoming leads to a more organized flow of the best leads (the "A" opportunities) first.

The effect is also felt in marketing. With company-by-company information on your prospects, the marketing team can start to tailor programs that will deliver more results for less investment in time and people. You can also improve your territory management. If you know the addresses and business niches of most of the likely prospects for the next twenty-four months, you can allocate sales channels to make sure each channel is calling on the best ones.

Figure 6-1. Changing the pipeline with an opportunity database.

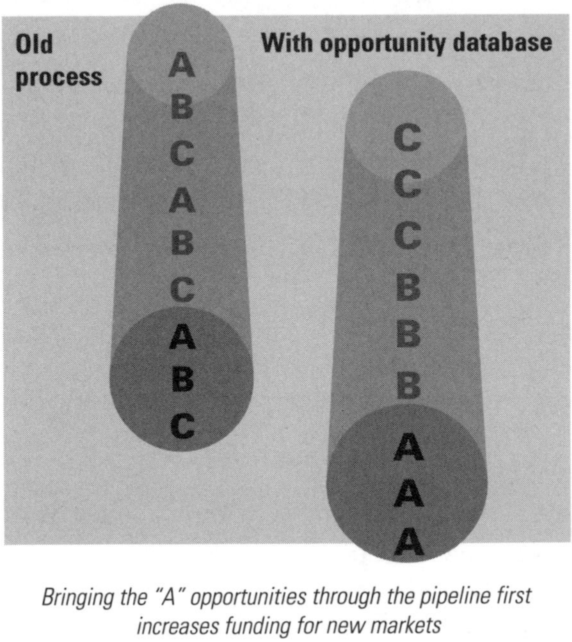

Bringing the "A" opportunities through the pipeline first increases funding for new markets

EXAMPLE

The opportunity database concept is straightforward—you identify as many prospects as you can and then market to them in
order, calling on the best ones first. If you want to fund growth,
this database is one of the best levers that you will ever have.

For example, in the 1990s, Aspect Telecommunications (now
Aspect Communications Corp.) competed in the market for call
center systems and software that answer or direct customer in-
quiries, such as when you call an airline or utility for information or help. Aspect was justly proud of the fact that it closed
more than half the deals it proposed, averaging $500,000 per
deal. At the time, all vendors combined sold 300 call center con-
tracts each calendar quarter in the United States. With its old
prospect management system, Aspect knew about a fraction of
those deals, missing some real opportunities.

With 300 deals happening in a given quarter, if the company
could tap just ten more opportunities per quarter in each of the
five regions, it could net an additional $25 million in revenue per
quarter with little additional resources. Knowing about the deals
allows the channels to deploy more efficiently without increasing sales costs. The key to gaining this benefit is in the market
knowledge that comes from the intelligent use of an opportunity
database. For Aspect, and perhaps for your business, enhanced
market knowledge:

►Allows sales representatives to call on the best prospects
first, maximizing revenue per person and territory per
month

►Enables sales managers to quantify the value of a given
territory and assign territories that are equal in opportunity, optimizing the profit per salesperson

▸Shows marketing exactly how to identify the niches with the highest potential, so it can then closely target the right markets and increase profit per customer

▸Gives the e-commerce group the information it needs to tailor its online strategies to prospective customers with the highest potential, maximizing revenue per person-day and dollars spent on e-commerce

▸Allows product marketing to aim future products more carefully, increasing the chances of success in product efforts without increasing the investments of time, people, or money

▸Helps financial analysts to price products to attract the portions of the market that will be more likely to pay for value, thereby maximizing return for the same sales and marketing effort

In other words, a business can deploy its channels more efficiently and gain more revenue and profits for the same sales, marketing, product, and finance staff. Opportunity databases are an excellent way to get the most resources in the least time and to help your business grow in a sustainable manner.

Identifying Common Denominators

The strategy to building an opportunity database is to identify all the likely prospects in a universe and then assign each prospect points according to the value of the opportunity the prospect represents to your business. The place to start is with common denominators.

Common denominators happen both intentionally and by accident. When certain customers are drawn to you because of effective marketing, you have intentionally created common denominators. If you make audio- and videoconferencing products, you may choose to target companies that have large travel budgets or many locations. You have chosen your customer sets.

You can accidentally arrive at customer sets as well. For instance, the sales teams of a phone system vendor can tell you that there are certain kinds of customers that are "theirs" while others "belong" to the competition. This can happen when your sales teams fall into the habit of selling to comfortable customer types or specific niches. It may not be what you intended, but it's what's comfortable for them. In the 1980s, a telephone systems vendor dominated the college and university market in the western United States not because the executive team chose that market, but because one salesperson enjoyed selling to campuses and was very successful at it. The sales representative got promoted and hired others who enjoyed the same prospective customers. Eventually, the vendor had a strong history in the postsecondary education market. The local sales team had unconsciously created common denominators for the entire company. This kind of serendipity happens frequently.

You may not like the common denominators that you have intentionally and unintentionally created. Even so, don't expend resources trying to change them. Instead, use the common denominators as strengths.

EXAMPLES

Aspect Communications, like most companies, sells well to customers that have certain common characteristics—for example, Aspect's customers buy specific computer hardware and software. Aspect's sales teams tend to sell in specific markets, such as the utility, retail, and financial services markets. To take advantage of those characteristics, Aspect's opportunity database includes every company in the United States that is likely to have the right meld of installed systems and those specific markets.

In your case, if you have found that you sell well to companies with widespread Windows NT deployments and that focus on the automobile industry, build a national (or international) database of prospective customers who have those common denominators. Instead of waiting for these customers to identify themselves to you, identify them first. By applying this concept, Aspect has been able to tailor its marketing efforts and direct its sales channels and teams to specific accounts instead of general areas. This targeted approach can bring any company quicker return, offering more resources to help it move into new markets in less time.

Another example is a leader in technology products used to improve meetings. This company (which prefers not to be identified or to tip off its competitors about its use of opportunity databases) dominates the sales of audio- and videoconferencing equipment to the Fortune 1000. With that market covered, the question is: "Who else might be a customer?" The universe of U.S. companies outside the Fortune 1000 is too large to address intelligently. However, a quick comparison of the characteristics of existing customers showed increased use of the company's products whenever there were multiple branches. When the company started to look at its list of customers outside the Fortune 1000, it found some common denominators for sales and installation success. Its next step was to build an opportunity database that explored the universe of midsize companies with many branches in certain industries. Such data on midsized and large companies is available now. You can take advantage of it at your convenience.

A third example is Dun & Bradstreet. Like any other company, D&B would prefer to have its sales teams call on the best leads first. In an experiment, one D&B region found that its best leads were companies that fit into very specific four-digit SIC codes, a clear set of common denominators. A consultant sorted the territory lists for the region and assigned priority to those common denominators. D&B not only found thousands of companies that had not yet been on a suspect list, it also increased sales per representative by almost 50 percent.

When you take advantage of such data to build an opportunity database, you'll have tens of thousands of these companies—a list that you can identify and then store on a laptop computer. By sorting that list against other common denominators, your company can direct its distributors to the prospects most likely to buy today's products.

Addressing Territory and Quota Integrity, and the Issues They Create

A benefit of an opportunity database is that you can use it scientifically to spread opportunity among the components of your channels and sales teams. Instead of assigning quota according to history, you can assign it by a logical point system. A high-end consumer products manufacturer would like to know if each of its fifteen distributors is working up to potential. With average sales of $5,000 per product, a little increase in effectiveness makes a big difference in revenue. For this company, the question has always been: How do we define "potential"?

The answer is to map the United States, by zip code, according to buying power for the company's products. The raw information for that mapping is available, but no one had assembled it in this way. The manufacturer can assign a point value to each zip code. That allows the company to know where the best opportunities are located throughout the United States. The next step is to map the zip code scores against a map that shows which distributor has which states and cities. That combined map can identify how the distributor or sales region is working against potential.

Figure 6-2 is a simple example that has a map of the United

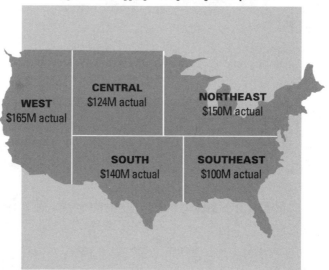

Figure 6-2. Mapping sales per region in year 1.

States broken into five fairly even regions—Southeast, Northeast, Central, South, and West—with sales numbers for each region for a given year. After an opportunity database is created and mapped to the same regions, you can derive a second map (Figure 6-3) to reveal regions that are either excelling compared to opportunity or selling below the actual opportunity.

Figure 6-3 shows that the Southeast region's team is working close to its potential while the Northeast region's team is working ahead of its potential. Though the Northeast's actual sales revenues are lower than the Western region, the database shows that they are doing more with less opportunity. The Western region's sales team has the best sales record, but it's not working up to the opportunity. Without this data, company executives might have moved resources to the wrong teams. This data allows the company to invest fewer resources in regions, but in a more scientific way. If the potential is significantly higher than results, a manufacturer can add resources to assist the distribu-

Figure 6-3. Mapping actual sales to opportunity.

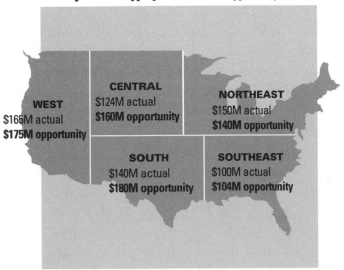

After an opportunity database is created and mapped to the regions, we can see that one region is selling well compared to opportunity, but that three regions are selling below the actual opportunity.

tor. The expectations of performance will increase at the same time, measured in quota. If the potential is not higher than results, the manufacturer can avoid wasting more time, people, and money in the territory.

When your team works toward territory and quota integrity, you should plan on dealing with other issues that this technique will bring to the surface. For instance, when you find a distributor who is doing well at maximizing opportunity, you may want to increase the territory that distributor can cover. That increase should come from the territory of the distributor who is not working to potential. In Figure 6-3, you might move more resources to the Southern region because the biggest opportunity is there. However, you will have moved from a historical view of territory sales to a scientific process.

The downside of this technique is that you may ruffle some feathers. Not all channels will welcome these measurements, so some adjusting may be required. For example, one distributor for high-tech capital equipment has convinced the manufacturer that its quota should be based on how it performed in recent years. With no evidence to the contrary, the manufacturer agreed. Then, when the manufacturer created an opportunity database, it found that the distributor had 18 percent of the national opportunity in its territory but carried only 10 percent of the quota every year. The manufacturer asked the distributor to carry more quota, and the distributor demurred. These conversations were quite active. Eventually the manufacturer realized that it could do better with its own people in the field. The distributor lost this franchise.

The result for the manufacturer? More direct customer contact and more fuel for the manufacturer's growth. It could spend about the same resources (i.e., time, people, and money) to get a higher return.

Assembling Your Team

A primary ingredient for success is involving the correct disciplines. To increase sales efficiency you need involve only the sales or channel organizations. However, if you want to gain time, people, and money across the organization, you will want to involve support from other functions as well, such as pricing, product development, marketing, field sales, and channels. Involving someone from pricing gives your business the chance to increase prices and margins when you start to target customers who perceive a greater need. Product development may play a key role in tailoring the product to meet the exact needs of the top prospects in the database; in the process, as you eliminate features that hold little value for those prospects, you also increase prices and drop costs. Marketing can find a way to present product to the prospective customer in a way that feels tightly tailored, because it is. Sales and distribution channels can add value by helping direct the best way to deliver the product. The opportunity database gives each discipline information to extract a little more fuel for growth from the same products and markets.

To build an opportunity database you must first assemble:

1. A guidance council, including:

▶A finance expert who can affect strategies for pricing and margins

▶A product development manager who can help direct the way that the company builds and presents its product(s)

▶A marketing manager who can direct strategies for more tightly tailored marketing efforts

▶A field sales manager who can help define how to organize the sales process around the new data

▶A channels manager who can help set strategies to organize the way the product moves through the distribution channels

2. An operational team, including:

▶A software expert who understands how to build an opportunity database

▶A programmer who understands databases

▶A manager who understands how your sales processes work

▶A fast desktop computer with plenty of hard disk capacity

Assembling an opportunity database is neither easy nor fast. You can develop the skills you need internally or call on two or three companies to perform the work for you.[1] For many companies, using an outside service will seem much less expensive than dedicating resources internally. This may be true, but be careful to look at the true costs in five key areas:

1. *Guidance.* You will want to assemble the guidance council from your own team no matter who does the actual work. The purpose of the council is not to do the work themselves, but to ensure that the action or operational team produces the right work product for your company. It would be a mistake to delegate that guidance to an outside firm.

2. *Data Analysis.* The work of massaging the data is highly specialized. You may have a person on staff who can learn the basics, experiment a little bit, and then do the work. Using that resource will avoid the cost of an outside expert, but you may find that it isn't worth the time that it would take. If your internal expert takes three months (probably half the time you'll really take) to get up to speed, that is a quarter of incremental revenue that you will forgo. While your staff person is learning, other companies may be winning business that should be yours.

3. *Database Creation.* People who can build opportunity databases are still rare. Your internal resource may be of great use to you doing something else. If so, you have an opportunity cost and a time and dollar cost. You can avoid that cost by "renting" the skill from an experienced service.

4. *Change Management.* If you do decide to revamp territories or change how you address your channels, you have both a time issue and a marketing cost. Those changes may be very lucrative, but they are difficult. Make sure that you budget time and dollars as you see the results of the database work.

5. *Program Redesign.* You will almost certainly have a set of marketing investments to make when you are done. You will have identified the best prospects in your universe, and you will want to tailor a program that takes best advantage of your new knowledge. To do this, you may want to eliminate other programs or add programs incrementally.

Getting the Next Level of Success

After your team delivers the opportunity database, ask it to take an important next step. If you have a 30 percent market share, build common denominators for the 70 percent you *don't* sell to, then build products to support a second opportunity database. Looking at your noncustomers may do more than help you find ways to expand your market. It may also show you a path to creating and dominating a new market.

The Practical Side: Eight Steps to an Opportunity Database

The process of building an opportunity database is not conceptually difficult. The difficulty is in the decisions and the database work. Although you have many options, here are eight recommended steps that can deliver an opportunity database.

Step 1: Go Back into the Data You Have for Your Existing Customers

Pull your records so that you can get the basic information in one data file. You want a significant sample—at least 20 percent to start. You'll need to have the data cleaned to correct addresses and remove duplications. If you do not already use them, you will need to add DUNS numbers or some other common identifier so that you can sort against data you import from outside sources. A DUNS number is a unique nine-digit identifier that Dun & Bradstreet assigns to each single business entity, and it has become a common and universally understood tool for identifying businesses and where they might fit into a corporate family. Since no two businesses should have the same number, a

DUNS number is a good identifier for a business, subsidiary, or branch stored in the opportunity database.

Step 2: Sort the Data for Common Denominators That Show Up in a Structured Sort

These common denominators could be four-digit SIC codes, common geographic tendencies, similar business family structures, similar size ranges by people or revenue, and so on. Direct your team members to be careful to ignore your company history and desires. They should not look for what marketing or sales wants to see. You want to discover what your customers are actually doing.

Step 3: Identify the Key Common Denominators for a Purchasing Decision

Avoid looking for budget information. The temptation of many sales teams is to talk about budget and cost savings. However, you can look at your own business to see that budgets and cost savings do not drive major purchases. Other business needs determine your purchases.

For example, a large regional accounting firm found that it was developing a lucrative business in managing inventory taxation issues. It was not intentional, just one of those accidental tendencies. The partners decided to leverage that newly discovered tendency and look for commonalities.

If they had looked for clients who had set aside budget for inventory tax work, they would have found no prospects. Instead, they looked beyond budgets and discovered that most of their clients bought special bar code labels before they did inventories or hired a specialist tax firm. The accounting firm went to the major inventory label companies and offered to rent their customer lists and comarket. What better way to get a view of future customers than to be there when they decide to do an inventory?

Since asking about budget is not the right tack, you should encourage your team to ask other questions. Four such questions are:

► What do our customers buy just before they buy from us?

► What markets do our customers use our products and services to enter?

► What markets will our customers be entering over the next twenty-four months?

► Why do our customer's customers buy from them?

Remember, don't ask your team—ask the customers. You will want to involve people from your sales, marketing, and finance functions, though, because as a group they will uncover trends that individual disciplines may miss. They will uncover common denominators that may include:

► Four-digit SIC codes (these codes can provide enough detail to learn that, for example, community colleges are good markets but universities are not)

► Organization structures (e.g., multiple divisions are a good or bad trait to sort for your customers)

► Revenue trends (e.g., growing customers do/do not gravitate to your product)

► Product purchases (e.g., your customers buy specialized bar code labels, sales force automation software, certain computer installations, or consulting services)

► Financial structures (e.g., your customers are primarily family-owned businesses)

▶Organization structures (e.g., your customers always have/ never have a human resources department)

▶Common target markets for your customers

These findings will be facts, not assumptions. Working from fact may settle some arguments; it will also make it easier to increase margins as you target your future customers.

STEP 4: ONCE YOU HAVE THE COMMONALITIES YOU WANT, LOOK FOR THE SAME DATA FOR YOUR COMPETITION'S CUSTOMERS

This step does not require buying your competitors' customer list—it can be done other ways. Several companies, such as Harte-Hanks Market Intelligence of San Diego (formerly known as ZD Market Intelligence and before that, Computer Intelligence) and Dun & Bradstreet, do extensive telephone surveys of business customers. These companies will sell you their lists sorted for such data as customer size, decision makers, names, phone numbers, number of installations, and so on. Since no vendor rigorously calls every company in the United States, even these lists will give you only a small portion of the marketplace. With this data expect a list of perhaps 25 percent of your prospective customers.

STEP 5: MATCH THE LIST AGAINST A STANDARD FOR IDENTIFYING LOCATIONS AND BUYERS

This step allows you to keep your data clean—avoiding the usual problem of having General Electric listed as GE, G.E., Gen'l E, and so on. A DUNS number is a good standard identifier to use in your database.

You cannot place too much emphasis on the value of having clean databases. Most national database suppliers allow inaccurate data—it is simply not worth the cost to correct all errors as they enter data. When you start sorting for commonalities, bad data quickly multiplies itself. You can drive the quality of your results below acceptable levels with only a few errors. The only answer is to clean the databases before you use them. It almost never works to let the data suppliers do it. You have to assume that you will spend time and money doing it yourself or hiring an expert third party.

Step 6: Buy the Information You Need from Other Databases That Highlight the Commonalities You Care About

If the commonalities are focused on computers and technology, you might call Harte-Hanks Market Intelligence. When the commonalities are focused on SIC codes, perhaps Dun & Bradstreet would be appropriate. If the commonality is from a product or service, consider the option of buying from or trading with other suppliers.

Step 7: Create Ranking Priorities for the Common Denominators

Create a scale from one to ten, with ten being the most value to your sales force. Then look at each common denominator and assign a value on the scale. The actual scoring will be specific to your business, but here are some examples:

Customer Common Denominator	Value
Buys inventory labels	8 points
Deploys a client/server-based architecture	4 points
Has more than four subsidiaries	6 points
Is located within 100 miles of a freight hub	2 points

Take the time to select some of your existing customers at random to check how they would rank. If your existing customers rate poorly in your scoring scheme, you have missed the target somehow. Most probably your team has assigned points for what they wish the customers would do, not what your customers are actually doing. Make adjustments and corrections to your rankings as necessary.

Step 8: Sort All the Lists Against the Common Denominators by DUNS Number and Point Value

The result will be a list of potential customers, ranked by relative value to you. In Aspect Communications' case, this was the 16,000 best prospects in the country. Then you can distribute the prospects in a way that helps your direct or distribution team focus on them. You have created an opportunity database.

Finding the Resources Inside the Business

You can find resources in other parts of your business by asking specific departments to supply them. If you wish to follow that strategy, consider starting with your information technology (IT) function. In many companies, IT absorbs more resources than almost any other part of the enterprise. Unfortunately, IT is one of the departments least likely to help you to create and dominate new markets. For this and other reasons, IT gets poor grades from chief executives.[2]

Technology requires ever more funding every year just to keep up with changes. Although IT is not the only function that can absorb as much resource as you have to invest, that department is a good place to start if you want to get more fuel for growth from the same resources. The same process applies to other departments as well. There is a fundamental principle at work here. The principle is that people who won't normally fund projects that the IT team values will cheerfully give you money for an effect they want. To apply that principle, start with the effect each department delivers.

What Is the Basic Function That You Deliver?

Start with a question for your IT team: What do you deliver to your customers—MIPS and digital dial tone, or market access and the ability to attract and hire new people? If you and your team define your products and services as an effect your customers want—the second answer—the team can find money outside its normal budget. This happens because IT customers rarely understand technical products; most users look at technology as a tool to contribute to the effects they need and therefore are willing to pay for.

IT can tap new resources for projects by defining technology products not as tools but as business effects—such as helping to open up new markets. If the IT team is delivering tools, their funding will be limited. No tool, no matter how strategic, is as compelling as the effect it helps to deliver. With that in mind, the team can look at several strategies to free resources for those effects. Five innovative strategies are:

1. Renting rather than buying

2. Billing users for the effects they get

3. Being a venture capitalist

4. Paying with currency other than cash

5. Funding your own dreams

Why Own?

The team can start with a basic question: Do we own our hardware now? If so, why? After all, your business "rents" contract programmers. It rents voice and data circuits. Why not let someone else own your hardware?

Buying PCs is traditional. In that model, your business gives them to the users and then tosses them out after a year or two. The focus is on the hardware, but do you want to supply your users with hardware or with the effect of that hardware?

If you want to supply the effect, your IT team can ask the PC vendor to create a technology upgrade program or package for your business. The vendor takes the hardware when it is obsolete and replaces it with newer hardware. You could structure this package as a rental or a lease, but either way the cost in your budget goes down this year and the risk of obsolete hardware gets shared with the people who made it. Many suppliers, including Compaq Computer, Dell Computer, Hewlett-Packard, and IBM have technology refreshing programs such as this. Some will rent out the software as well.

When your IT team rents, it may incur a greater total cost in dollars than it would by buying. In return, however, it gains the option of delaying the payment over time and using present-day cash and time for other projects. It gains the time-savings from being able to walk away from obsolete hardware. When the IT team rents or leases a million-dollar capital investment, it becomes only a few hundred thousand dollars in the current year's budget. That frees up cash for you to explore and create new markets. In effect, your vendor is financing your growth into new markets.

Renting is a tradeoff, though. To the financial analysts, it is a calculation of the opportunity cost of money. A transaction that saves a little cash and time may be valuable in helping your company enter a new market. That is a transaction you want to foster.

Bill Your Users for the Effect They Get

Even if you do not stop owning hardware, your IT team can take a different proposition to your users. It can ask users if they are willing to pay for the effects they want out of the incremental savings they'll generate.

To show how this strategy might work, start with the safe bet that someone will ask IT to do an interesting but unbudgeted project. They will suggest that it's a great idea because it will save more than it costs. The IT team's normal response is negative. Ask for a change in that response by encouraging the IT team to consider the project as an investment. If the senior IT management thinks the idea is interesting, IT can take the users up on the offer. When that happens, be sure that both the requesting department and IT share the risk.

A real example comes from the history of voice-mail systems. From the start, users said they would save a fortune in time and money if they installed voice mail systems. However, IT usually got left with the costs. A few early adopters said yes to voice mail, but those IT functions asked the requesting departments to fund part of the cost. The conversation went something like this: "If you are willing to cut $25,000 out of your budget for two years, we'll buy you a $50,000 system right now." Some users said yes. They were the ones who got voice-mail service more quickly. The same model can work today. Whenever they get a special request, the IT team can ask the requester to help fund the project with time, people, and money.

Since the objective is to free up resources for market expansions, the IT budget should not be the funding device. Instead, look to vendors or third parties to fund the systems. Consider the example of the airline industry. Engine suppliers may fund leases for air carriers to help them buy whole planes, knowing that engine sales will result. The engine companies do it to help create a new market. Many IT vendors will do the same.

California's Franchise Tax Board (FTB) used this idea to fund a project the legislature would not. The FTB (the agency that collects taxes in California) knew it could pay for the $50 million investment with additional collections that the system would enable. As compelling as the case was, the legislature would not set aside that much money.

The FTB went to a finance company and the vendors of the proposed system. The offer to the vendors was easy: If they would find a way to fund it, they would get the deal. That meant some risk for these suppliers. They were betting that they could help the state collect more than the $50 million. If the state failed to collect the money, the vendors would lose some or even all of the investment.

Ultimately, two vendors formed groups and took different phases of the project. When they turned the system on, it didn't work as planned. It worked better. With so much at stake, the vendors did an excellent job for the IT customer. The result? The project paid off more quickly than forecast and generated a profit for the FTB and for the vendors. The FTB has an important positive effect and a new system. All without a budget hit.

Be a Venture Capitalist

If your company takes marketplace risks, why shouldn't IT? Why not have IT make a special offer to a peer department? IT agrees to install the effect the department manager dreams of (but could not get approved) and lets the department pay over time. In return, IT gets 25 percent of the amount above the forecasted savings or revenue. The department keeps the forecasted return and 75 cents of every dollar above it. IT gets supplemental income as a bonus for imagination and extra work. Eventually, IT becomes a venture capitalist.

The City of Philadelphia used this strategy at the height of its fiscal crisis in 1992. The city created an ongoing capital pool (called the Productivity Bank) and "loaned" money to internal projects that would pay back more than the loan. It demanded that each project return at least $2 for every $1 the bank lent, a difficult hurdle. In five years the bank turned $20 million in loans into $59.6 million in cost savings and increased revenue.

Philadelphia decided to let departments borrow from a Productivity Bank to buy the effects of information technology. This formed an off-budget capital pool for technology without taking money from the IT or general funds. The hard part is that the departments had to return twice the money they borrowed. On the other hand, they could return it out of savings or revenue. This alternate funding project worked because the people involved focused on the effect of the funding, not the technology they were buying.

As an example, in the early 1990s officials never really knew how many city vehicles they had on the streets, which made it difficult to manage this expensive asset. The Office of Fleet Management asked for funding to fix this situation, but money wasn't available in the general fund. So the department went to the Productivity Bank and asked for a little less than $2 million. With the money, the department installed a system that tells controllers where each car is, when the next preventive maintenance check on the car should be scheduled, and when the city should retire the vehicle. This tool has no real magic; it is an information management program applied to a place where there were few controls. It worked. The system saved the city $3.9 million in the first five years. The department paid back the bank, and the city is still saving money.

Asking a department to become a venture capitalist may seem to be heresy, but if it worked for a city on the verge of bankruptcy, why not for your organization? Ask your IT department, or any service department, to try it.

Don't Pay with Cash

Most department budgets are based on money, but the managers have other forms of "currency" to invest. Look at what else departments have to sell or trade. IT may have information, services, market access, testing facilities or other things you can trade for capital equipment and software. Using those resources can conserve cash.

An example is a KPMG/Microsoft joint venture that started as a cash purchase. KPMG Consulting, Inc. had decided to buy intranet software from Netscape Communications. The consulting firm realized, though, that it had information and market presence that Microsoft Corp. wanted, and Microsoft wound up paying KPMG, as a customer, to get access to that information and market presence. Both KPMG and Microsoft wound up winners, even as Microsoft ended up funding part of the customer's installation.

Look at your own IT department for alternative currencies. Does the team collect data on the performance of your systems and network? That data may be valuable to others. For example, most of your technology vendors have teams that develop new products. They work from what they think happens in the real world. They know that the model may not be right, but they have no real way to test it. Vendor development teams would love to have access to the real-world information you have collected.

Fund Your Own Dreams

In the scenarios we have discussed thus far, the IT department is funding the dreams of colleagues in other departments or organizations. Why stop there? Each department has its own goals and objectives that it can foster with innovative funding. Instead of asking the team to do more with less, ask the members to "tell me your dream and what you would cut from your budget to fund that dream."

Identify the dream for the whole department, and ask everyone to help with the tradeoffs needed to make it a reality. It does not need to be an even trade. A head of a department who needs to find an additional 10 percent in resources can ask the whole team to work out how to conserve 20 percent. When the team knows that it gets to spend part of the savings, it changes how it looks at resources.

Advantages to Funding Growth Internally to Support New Markets

There are many other ways to fund your growth internally. You'll gain many advantages when you do so. You can avoid the pressures of finding time, people, and money outside the business and eluding the cost of interest on loans and investments. Consider an even more important advantage: When you fund from your own operations you make your best people more available to your new markets. Freeing up your people and their time is more important than any money that you might save, and it sets a precedent for how to do business. It makes your effort to create a new market more efficient.

Finally, the more you streamline your old business, the more likely your team is to work to streamline your new business as well. You can improve your existing operations as you create and dominate a new market.

The Results to Your Business

Quantifying your opportunity reduces the risks of growth and fuels your future. Overall, a business will get three incremental forms of fuel for growth from the opportunity database.

Three Fuels for Growth

1. *Extra Time the Business Can Use to Explore and Open New Markets.* By using an opportunity database your best people will be more focused in their work, allowing them to avoid time investments in marginal markets.

2. *People.* When your people use opportunity databases to target customers very clearly, they can take that skill and experience into new markets. Learning to focus helps identify key markets in less time

3. *Incremental Profit from Sales.* When you sell more and discount less, that profit will be cash you can use to create and dominate your next market without stealing from the current one.

7

What Role Does the Customer Play?

Many of the best ideas to create new markets come from great minds that see a future need and find a way to satisfy that need. Unfortunately, this approach fails more often than it works. One common denominator for successfully creating new markets is to involve the customer. The problem is that while involving the customer makes intellectual sense, it is counterintuitive for most managers.

Internally Driven Versus Customer Driven

For many business owners and managers, great ideas well up from within. They represent a plan or need that the manager feels strongly about and wishes to solve. The vision is intense, and the best visions are transferable. Steve Jobs had a vision of an "insanely great" desktop computer that would free people by helping them work more creatively. He was able to express that vision and created a substantial market with his company and the Apple Macintosh computer. Apple Computer dominated the market long enough to make a real difference.

Don Estridge at IBM Corp. had a different vision for a similar product, a desktop computer that would help office people work more independently. Estridge's team created a new corporate market, which it called professional computing, and proceeded to dominate that market for years. The team that built Microsoft Corp. had a vision that complemented Estridge's. Bill Gates, Paul Allen, and Steve Ballmer saw an opportunity to tie disparate software programs together into a single platform on the personal computer. That integration created a new market, and Microsoft has dominated the market ever since then.

Sam Walton and his team envisioned large retail stores in small towns offering low prices and competitive service. Wal-Mart Stores, Inc. has since dominated each geographic market it entered, changing the competitive retail landscape in each area.

Each of these ideas came from true visionaries who were willing to take a risk and invest a great deal of time. Sometimes they added their personal fortune (be it small or large). They all became famous, and thousands of others have tried to follow their footsteps. However, most followers failed. Why?

Starting with a vision is a high-risk plan. You rarely hear of LOMAC (Logical Machine Corp., which made a PC that could recognize and respond to voice commands, closed in the 1980s) or Osborne Computer (which produced a portable computer that was highly regarded but sold poorly; the company closed shortly after it shipped its first products). Few people remember VisiCalc (the initial spreadsheet software for Apple computers) or Ashton-Tate (which made dBASE database software and now no longer exists). Each of these companies, at least, was able to make a splash. For every VisiCalc or Ashton-Tate, though, you can find hundreds of others that tried and sank without a ripple.

In every effort at a new market, you take your best shot, and sometimes it works. Not even the best in the business world are infallible. A case in point is Cisco Systems, Inc. Cisco has been a market creator and leader from the time that it first started to build products that power the Internet. When you log onto the Net, or onto a company network, routers and switches convert your messages to packets and convey your data to and from the network. Cisco created the market for these routers and switches, and the company dominates that market today. Cisco has been better at reading customer requirements than most companies, and it has kept its focus. Even so, the company has missed several times. In April 2001, the company discontinued an optical router that it acquired in 1999 as part of its initial foray into the optical networking market. " 'The market was growing too slowly for us to maintain the investment,' said Carl Russo, vice president of Cisco's optical networking business unit. . . . The Monterey product called for a new way for carriers to build networks, something they're not willing to do with the slowing U.S. economy."[1] Ultimately, the company was forced to write off nearly a half-billion dollars in optical equipment, including lasers and modulators.[2]

The problem is simple: What appeals to the inventor does not necessarily appeal to the market. The question is how to make the appeal more predictable. When you approach the effort to create a new market, you have three basic strategies, and all three have difficulties:

Strategy	Difficulties
Shape the market	Low barriers for competition
	Often ineffective with prospective customers
Predict the market	Often inaccurate
	Entire effort wasted if a mistake in timing occurs

Strategy	Difficulties
Ask your customers for help	Expensive in terms of time, people, and dollars
	May not yield the answers you want
	May downplay products

Shaping the Market

Product managers have the assignment to both shape the product and mold the market to accept that product. Shaping is the essence of positioning—that is, of working to have customers view the need and the product in the way you do.

The sale of nuclear power plants has been, in some ways, a process of positioning by suppliers, their competitors, and third parties (such as environmentalists and local residents) that want to become involved in where or whether to place the plants. One group of marketers would like the public to recognize an ever-increasing need for clean and safe power. The positioning is that the need is there and nuclear is the lowest-risk alternative. At the same time, other groups suggest that coal, natural gas, renewable resources, or energy conservation are much better solutions. They would position nuclear as quite risky. Irrespective of the validity of the arguments, all these advocates are working to shape the market.

The difficulty in shaping the market comes in two forms. One is that you will have competition in positioning. As with the nuclear power example, anyone can try to affect the market with positioning efforts. Often, in that kind of competition, the winner is not chosen on the merits of the product but the merits of the positioning. The second difficulty comes in getting acceptance by customers. Customers are seldom willing to let you lead them with positioning.

Predicting the Market

If we could accurately predict the market, Osborne Computer would never have released its C/PM-based portable business computer as a commercial product when it did, the Edsel would have stayed on the drawing board, and the Apple Newton would have remained a prototype. Predicting the desire of customers is both difficult and dangerous to the health of your company.

In the late 1990s and early 2000s, many companies invested heavily in the predicted demand for web-enabled telephones. The idea seemed attractive. Cell phone users could surf the Web, send e-mail, or get stock or weather reports on the display on their phone. Since these are not revenue-generating ideas, companies also invested in creating web-enabled commerce applications for phones. Some applications were based on a proposed standard known as Wireless Application Protocol (WAP); some were proprietary. Analysts and marketers coined the term *m-commerce* (for mobile commerce) to differentiate the projects from electronic commerce. Amazon.com was reported to have dedicated thirty people to developing a set of m-commerce applications.

Yet all this activity and investment of resources have not created a market. Customers have simply not wanted to use cell phones to buy books or surf the Web, and many companies that formed to take advantage of WAP technologies have had to change their charter or fold. Amazon has reduced its staffing for m-commerce considerably. If your business had invested in m-commerce in 2000, you wouldn't have seen any return in twelve to twenty-four months.

Timing is also critical for this strategy to work. If the m-commerce market happens two years later than predicted, you may have wasted your work. Correctly predicting a market but missing the timing is just as dangerous as predicting the wrong market. One way to increase the chances of success is to ask your customers to help.

Asking Your Customers to Help

If the best path to new markets is to involve customers, what role should the customer play in defining a market? The fact that the customer does not know that the market exists makes this question even more complicated.

First, you must decide whether your business wants to enter markets that are customer driven or internally driven (i.e., defined by what your team thinks is right). You may be tempted to answer automatically that "we want to be customer driven." However, that answer is not so clear when you actually go to implement a plan.

You can't just ask prospective customers what they want in a new market. They don't know. If they did, it wouldn't be a new market anymore. The market for fax machines is a good example of this phenomenon. When the machines were first introduced, very few companies were willing to spend $1,000 for the devices. Although several large companies with very smart people tried to shape this market, prospective customers just did not want to bother at that price point. When asked, they said no. However, when other companies introduced moderately priced machines, customers did what they had said they wouldn't—they bought fax machines. Today, these devices are in nearly every business and in many homes in the United States.

Similarly, customers told the America Online (AOL) team that they did not need an online service. General consumers could not quite understand what it was to be "online," or why they would care. If you asked average consumers if they wanted to have an online presence, the answer was, "Why?" However, if you asked if they might like to join an informal group of people to chat, or have a way to send quick notes to family members without having to buy stamps and mail letters, consumers responded positively. Customers didn't care about the product—they cared about the effects that online services could provide. Steve Case, AOL's CEO, started to become available to customers through electronic mail and chat sessions to ask them what they thought would make a difference in the service. AOL would repeatedly suggest product ideas that made sense to the internal development team. Consumers would frequently say no to the products, but yes to the effects. Instant messaging did not "sell" as a product, but it took off once customers realized it was a great way to communicate with friends and coworkers.

Asking customers what they would buy is especially treacherous. They may not give you the answers that you like, and then you have to adjust for customers who have no stake in the output of your work. It's also expensive in terms of time, people, and dollars. Once you have a product idea, you only have so many weeks or months before you must get it out the door. Asking the wrong questions of your customers can delay that time significantly, especially if the answers are not what you have been developing.

The lesson is that if you rely on customer advice concerning a specific product, you are likely to be staring at the wrong answer. You *can't* rely on customers to tell you what kind of product they might want, but you *can* rely on them to explain their problems—and you may find that customers will pay for solutions that would eliminate those problems. When you ask customers to help you, start with problems.

Lessons from the Field: Gauss

Many companies strive to create and dominate new markets. Sometimes market creation can be as simple as taking a great idea and hoping that you can find the customers who will adopt it. Sometimes that works. Netscape helped create a market for web browsers. On the other hand, you may remember that IBM, Sears, and GE all tried to start and prevail as national Internet service providers. None succeeded. That lack of success often comes when businesses have internal reasons to want a new market to exist, then find that those reasons do not translate to customers.

One technology company, Gauss, built a plan to let its customers drive product and marketing requirements.[3] This section offers suggestions for how you might adapt that plan to your business. There are three fundamental steps to letting your customers help build your new markets:

1. Make sure that your business understands the problem as the customer sees it.

2. Find a way to ask the prospective customers how they define success for solving this problem, even if they do not understand the issue itself.

3. Quickly bring a product to market that clearly addresses those success criteria. Remember, the product includes everything the customer experiences, not just the technology.

To apply these three steps, let's look at the problem of managing content on websites.

Understanding the Problem as the Customer Sees It

As the Web has grown more popular, managing websites has become dramatically more difficult. Many sites are on internal company networks (intranets); some run on private intercompany networks (extranets). Many more are public Internet sites.

With the volume of sites comes the need to distinguish one from another.

Customers want to differentiate sites. One way to differentiate is to continually add fresh and interesting material. As sites add more content, the sheer volume of pages and frequency of updates makes them difficult to manage. One answer is to use more people to manage them. Webmasters have that role and manage the flow of content from the original creators to the website. The webmaster posts the content correctly and enforces the rules that each company creates to control the look and feel of its sites. However, most companies cannot find and hire enough webmasters. As a result, getting content on the Web quickly and correctly becomes problematic. This can affect your customers, who will notice if your site's content is old or inaccurate.

Gauss (a company based in Hamburg, Germany) chose to solve the problem of keeping websites current by creating products to:

1. *Make it easy to move ideas from the minds of people to the websites, where the ideas can be useful.* The company's products allow a content creator or collaborative group to originate content on the site without manual intervention by the webmaster. Content creators work in the software programs with which they are comfortable, then automated systems send the information (e.g., documents, graphics, pictures, or streams of video) to the people who need to approve it.

2. *Make that same information easy to find and access.* Once content is put on a website, software programs are used so the site is aware of the new content and can find it quickly. The software also presents the information in a way that most people can easily use.

The Gauss team knew that they were not alone in seeing the potential market for these content management products. More than a dozen companies in the United States hoped to supply products that address these two issues. However, despite the ready availability of these tools, few customers buy them. Instead, companies with complex websites prefer to create their own content management procedures or do without. It's an example of how the availability of good technology does not make a market. Gauss decided to address the market differently by asking how the customer sees the problem of web management.

The typical strategy is to ask buyers what they want. In a new market, that strategy doesn't work. If you asked horse riders in the mid-1800s if they would buy a car, most would have said no. If you described this noisy machine that needed a strange fuel and almost nonexistent roads, you would have been presented with looks of sheer astonishment. This was true for those trying to sell the idea of the Web in the early 1990s and, it turns out, content management software in 2000 and 2001. The ideas make no sense to nontechnical buyers, yet most of the people with the problem are nontechnical. How do you ask customers about the issue without getting into the technology? If you decide to let customers drive your specifications and marketing, the lessons from this example can be very useful.

Gauss worked with a specialist telephone research firm (the Leeds Company in Westlake Village, CA) to create a survey. To get information as the prospective customer sees it, Leeds conducted live, phone surveys.

The tendency is to ask about products, and in fact the first questions did just that. The first lesson became apparent almost immediately: No one knew what Leeds's callers were talking about. Few prospective customers had any idea what this new product category of content management was, and they didn't care to get an explanation of how it worked. In response, Leeds rewrote the questions, asking what kept the Web from being more useful to the business, not what products and features the customers might want.

If you are doing a survey of your customers, make sure that you lead with the problem, not the product. These questions make a good starting point:

▶When you think about how your business uses the Internet, what problems keep you up at night?

▶Where are you putting most of your resources?

▶Why do people use your intranet/Internet sites? Why should they? Why is there a difference?

▶If you could fix any two things about how the Internet works for your department, what would they be?

Since they were looking for problems, the Gauss team chartered Leeds to cover a broad range of business units. While the IT department might be the ultimate buyer, Gauss also wanted interviews with marketing, finance, human resources, sales, and other departments. Whenever possible, the Gauss team wanted to get interviews with people who ran business units.

Agreed-on definitions were also a problem at first. What is a department? When does a department become a business unit? After much discussion, the team decided not to set firm rules. As you follow this path, do not try to define a business unit too tightly. Let the prospective customers do that for their own company. Each company will look at organizational structure differently. Your goal is not to tell them that they are wrong, but to understand what they are thinking and why. This approach, combined with the broad nature of the questions, lengthens the phone calls. Although traditional telemarketing has a focus on completing calls as quickly as possible, this form of survey work is different. Here you should work to get more thorough answers. Allow the calls to take as long as they need. In the Gauss survey, some calls took thirty minutes or more, but they delivered a wealth of detail.

You can take the opportunity to start each call with the CEO. In this survey, several CEOs took the time personally to respond. The good news is that these CEOs feel frustration at the way their business uses information and the Web. The bad news is that they are indifferent to the product differentiation issues that most vendors are promoting. These vendors took a lot of time to build differences that the CEOs did not care about. It's no wonder that most companies didn't buy content management.

Using Customer Success Criteria

As the survey results began to flow, Gauss and Leeds started to look for the customer's success criteria. This was the most important surprise. The answers were not what the teams from either company expected. There were few concerns about cost, technical issues, or how webmasters worked. The top four concerns expressed by customers were:

1. *Time.* The worst problem is that it takes too long for information to get onto the company's website. Business units were finding that it could take up to forty-five days from the moment an individual contributor created content until the moment that it became visible on the internal or external website. Often, the material was stale by the time it got to the end-users. For many business units, stale is unacceptable.

2. *Ease of Setup and Use.* Many business units were looking for a solution that would have out-of-the-box functionality. Just as important, the respondents requested solutions that didn't

require the content creators to use new tools or learn new programming.

3. *Fitting the Tool to the Business.* The respondents were clear that they did not want to change their business to use the tools. To quote one print executive, "I just want to get back to publishing books!" Managers wanted solutions that did not disrupt the flow of the business.

4. *Control.* Many business units and IT departments had real concerns about control of the content. These issues ranged from quality control to concerns that an employee might simply put the wrong information on the site or that the content needed to comply with a regulatory requirement.

The most important lesson of the entire project may be that most of the vendors in the web content management market had been self-centered. They had been focusing on success criteria that matched the vision of their company instead of the criteria set by the customers. This created a mismatch, and made it harder for prospective customer to decide to enter the market and buy any of the products.

Gauss's competitors created key messages, but not necessarily the messages that addressed the questions customers were asking. Many prospective customers were reluctant to invest in a software package that cost, on average, well over $100,000 without knowing that the product would solve the problem as *they* saw it. It would be advantageous to define the product so that the customer can fit it to the needs of his business. The product set and messages should include discussions of how to exercise the control that customer wishes. To create the market for content management solutions successfully, you want to build messages that address working in Internet time and making your product as easy to use as possible. Here are examples of internally driven messages (or messages that have not worked) and customer-driven messages that are more likely to succeed:

Internally Driven Messages	Customer-Driven Messages
"The only database-driven, enterprisewide publishing solution available today that is truly content based."	"Move your ideas to the Web in Internet time, not bureaucratic time."
"Controls the development, management, and deployment of business-critical websites."	"Up and running in hours, without IT."
"Whoever finds and keeps the most customers wins."	"Adapt the software to your needs, not vice versa."
"E-business or no business."	"Who controls the content on your site in real time? You do."

This may seem like a flash of the blindingly obvious, but the products and marketing show that these facts are not clear to the companies that are trying to create and then dominate the web content management market.

Applying What You Learn

When you ask your customers for help, the good news is that you know what the customers think. The bad news is that you may find that your technically elegant solution or product may not meet the needs that the customers state and therefore won't build a market.

Above all, the need to bring a product to market quickly will drive a company's design decisions. Most vendors design their solutions to leverage the technical skills of the supplier, yet those designs may be at odds with the success criteria for your customers. As Regis McKenna points out, there is a difference between being first to market and being first to market acceptance. You cannot assume that what is easy for the vendor is right for the customer. Let's look at three decision points from this project and how the Gauss team chose to address each issue.

Decision 1: Require a Database? Building a content management product quickly is much easier for the supplier if the customer will buy and use a separate structured database product. However, customers prefer to scatter most of their information across hundreds or thousands of files and computers. The process of moving all that data to a centralized database is both disruptive and time-consuming.

Most of the vendors in this market ask the customer to accept that cost as well as the delays. A speedy implementation of a product, for the user, is not possible if someone has to find and move all that data to the new database. It means forgoing the simplicity, for the supplier, of requiring a special database to make it easier for the nontechnical user. This decision may appear difficult unless you look at what the customer asks. Then the decision gets easy.

Decision 2: Web Tools or Office Tools? Most web technology suppliers will ask content collaborators to use web tools (i.e., forms or templates) to enter information and manage their files and data. However, most of the people who create content use programs that they are comfortable using, such as Microsoft Word (for word-processing documents), Lotus (for spreadsheets), or Adobe Photoshop (for graphics). When you decide to let the customer drive your specifications, you decide to let them use the software with which they are familiar. That does not usually include web forms.

Decision 3: Support Older Hardware? For a supplier, it is easier to build products that run only on new hardware. The problem is that many companies have and use every kind of computer, from PCs to a mainframe. Analysts have noted that 70 percent of all the world's data resides on computers with which most vendors' products do not work. Customers are not interested in changing computers to make it easier for the supplier. Creating products that play well with most common installations is more difficult for a vendor, but that's what will work best for customers.

Differentiating Product in the Eyes of the Prospective Customer

We often talk about differentiating a product or service. To increase sales and speed adoption of your product, you want to build that differentiation on how the prospective customers understand their problems. The most common question, then, may be: Which customer?

Inside the customer's business, you may discover that different stakeholders view the problem in completely different ways. In their work on content management, Gauss and Leeds found that many marketing departments and CEOs perceived the problem in terms of time-savings, ease of use, control, and the tool's fit with the business need. However, many IT departments in the same companies didn't think there was a problem at all.

Many technology vendors differentiate their products to meet the needs of IT teams. Meeting the needs of the technical staff is comfortable for the vendor, which is itself usually staffed by technically oriented teams. That comfort extends to the technical customers. However, the business units have different perceptions of the issues. The same is true for advertising campaigns. Outside firms design many advertisements that the customer's executives will be comfortable with. That doesn't mean the ads will work in the real world.

What the customer-driven process showed Gauss was that

corporate marketing departments value time over money. These people want to work in "Internet time" and find that the existing processes don't allow that. Without asking, the Gauss team might have missed that key product differentiation. Without understanding business managers' different perceptions of the issues, IT might have bought the product but been unable to get it adopted by the business units.

To avoid rejection by the technology users, Gauss is doing what many companies need to do. It is using differentiations that vary between stakeholders in the customer companies. Industries and companies do not decide to buy your products. Groups of stakeholders do that. It may be harder to do, but it pays to market to customers at that level of granularity.

When Gauss decided to let the customer drive the way its products are focused and presented, the company chose the more difficult path. However, if the customers truly feel that there is a problem and want to solve it, the company that can resolve that problem is the company best positioned to build a market.

The Customer and New Markets

When you involve customers in designing new markets, you increase the costs to enter that market. It takes more time, more people, and more money to work with prospective customers. It also requires the discipline to discuss problems without solving them, and without discussing (i.e., selling) products. For those costs you gain only one benefit: the ability to get to market acceptance much more quickly. That benefit is immense and can make all the trouble worth your while.

8

Building and Dominating Markets Through Involvement

Creating a new market does not mean that you will dominate it. Perrier does not dominate the market for bottled water. CompuServe does not dominate the market for online services. Osborne Computer does not dominate the market for portable computers. There's considerable work for you to do between creating the market and being able to dominate it (and reap the emotional and fiscal rewards from that domination). After you create a new market, your business has to find a way to build that market so that it becomes large enough to support itself. Otherwise, you have nothing to dominate.

There are several pitfalls to watch out for when building a

Note: Portions of this chapter were originally published as "Wireless Network Lessons," by Peter Meyer, in the (Vol. 47:3, April 2001) issue of *Business & Economic Review*, published by the Division of Research, The Moore School of Business, The University of South Carolina (pp. 28, 29). They have been modified for this book. Reprinted with permission.

new market (see Figure 8-1). Once you have launched your products and services, what are the chances that your products will be 100 percent what your customers want? Those chances are very poor. By following the suggestions presented so far in this book, you will be close. Osborne Computer and Compu-Serve were close. Being close is not enough to sustain a market.

When you are on target with what your customers want, will the target change? With complete certainty. The very creation of the market and the presence of your products will change the way potential customers see your products. What was fine last week will be the platform on which you improve and build the next level of products.

As you improve your products and services, you have an-other issue to wrestle with: Will your customers stay loyal to you? Only if being loyal to you is the same as being loyal to themselves. To get that fidelity, you need to program loyalty into your offerings from the first contact with the customer. The more your customers associate their own satisfaction with your product, the more loyalty you engender.

Figure 8-1. Three pitfalls between market creation and success.

PITFALL	RESULT
Launching is slightly off target.	Market does not take off; someone else makes the correction and creates the market.
The target will move immediately.	Market stalls after take off; someone else recognizes the change and grows the market.
Customer loyalty to you is always bounded by customers' loyalty to themselves.	Customers make decisions to support themselves instead of your business. They may not choose to install and use your product out of pure self-interest.

One solution to all of these pitfalls is to provide ways for the customer to become personally involved in the product. You can, and should, use customers to define and then build new markets. Customers can be more than a commodity to be directed and addressed as buyers. They can be active in helping your business to create and dominate new markets more quickly. You may feel that from an engineering and product design perspective, customers are passive. From a business-building orientation, though, they should be active partners. This alliance is not just altruism on your part. It will also help you to reduce the risk inherent in creating and dominating new markets.

A fully transparent product does not engender as much loyalty as a product that is visible to the user and that the user can tailor to fit his needs. Customer involvement also tells you where you are off target, and when the target is moving.

Involving Customers to Increase Your Opportunities

Whenever you attempt to create a new market, you won't know what will sell. When you don't know what to sell, the temptation is to return to the known and to develop and sell the technology or product that you control and understand.

Moving beyond that is risky. Your best people can bet your business, but you are still gambling. How do you hedge your bet? One way is to spur new customers to redefine your product as they use it. Encourage users to tailor the product to their own use, even if you have no idea what that use is.

Note: An overview of this section originally appeared in the author's book *Warp-Speed Growth* (New York: AMACOM, 2000) and in the (Vol. 46:3, April 2001) issue of *Business & Economic Review,* published by the Division of Research, The Moore School of Business, The University of South Carolina. Reprinted with permission.

The Trap of Core Competencies

Involving customers runs counter to most product and technology development efforts, with good reason. When you know a market, you can use that knowledge to invest in long-term strategies to deploy technologies that won't cover their costs for years or decades. However, your experience can be a substantial limitation in a new market if you become defined by your previous expertise. Working from core competencies is useful when you want to expand your position in competitive markets, but the past may hamper your growth into new businesses. Your core competency can blind you to new opportunities.

Motorola, Inc. based its future on the company's competency in analog cellular phone technology. It provided a substantial revenue stream, but cost the company access to a growing market extension. Like many decisions, it was a gamble. The question is whether you can improve your odds by moving beyond your core competency.

Looking at new markets often means changing the management team's focus. An internal focus is critical for sustainable success in competitive markets, and it reflects your core competency and strength. However, an external focus is what you need for markets that do not yet exist.

Advancing technology does not create new markets. Bell Laboratories had the transistor for years before Sony Corp. used it to make a new market for personal stereos. Xerox Corp. had a mouse-driven, graphical user computer interface for years before Apple Computer adopted the technology to create a market for personal desktop publishing. Companies make new markets. Technology's role is merely to help deliver the services and products for that new market. In new markets you can do better by downplaying technology and letting individual customers define their experience for themselves, and for you. With that capability, you can emulate America Online, LEGO, Celgene

Corp., the Polaroid instant camera, and other products that have dominated new markets.

Products That Let Consumers Define the Experience

Involving customers so that they can define their own experience with a product or service is a common denominator among many companies that create and dominate markets. There are at least two common denominators for success:

▶*Self-Tailoring.* The user can simply and easily adapt the product to individual needs that the supplier never considered. Instant photography has been a useful tool for builders, artists, and doctors as well as for photographers. Users can tailor Palm personal digital assistants to give directions during a bicycle ride or to operate as a remote control. Just as important, these adaptations deliver instant gratification. The user can make meaningful changes and see them occur.

▶*Ease of Use.* The products use advanced technologies, but do not ask the users to master that sophistication.

America Online (AOL) exemplifies a product that offers both self-tailoring and ease of use. The product, which is a combination of a service and a software package, presents an easy-to-use interface that allows each individual to define how AOL works for that user. The company encourages customers to think of themselves as part of the service, and calls them members. There's "My AOL" and "My Files." As an AOL member you know when "You've Got Mail" or "You've Got Pictures." Users can tailor the primary screen for their own custom channels and personalized websites and control the materials their children can download from the Internet. Each AOL member decides each change. Each member can determine his or her own appearance.

AOL's behind-the-scenes technology is sophisticated and complicated, but that complexity is invisible to the member. AOL has learned that users do not care how the tailoring takes place, only that it can be done quickly and easily.

Instant cameras introduced instant gratification and increased personal tailoring to photography. You'd take a picture, and if you didn't like it, you could shoot it again right away. The person holding the camera had control and immediate satisfaction. Today, many professional photographers still use instant cameras to show clients how the final shot will look. They set up the expensive, slow, and delayed-gratification equipment and then take a few instant shots. If the instant shots please the photographer and client, the shoot proceeds. If the instant shots show a problem, they adapt immediately. Feedback and tailoring of the work are immediate.

LEGO plastic bricks are a classic product built around customer involvement. A child (of any age) who creates with LEGO blocks is self-tailoring the experience. Half the sales of the company's Mindstorms products in 1999 were reportedly to adults wanting to built their own creations/robots. The company boasts that it has made thirty-three LEGO bricks for each person alive in the world. Much of that growth comes from the ability of individuals (of any age) to create their own experience with the basic product.

This ability to let the user define the experience was intentionally built into the instant camera and the LEGO block, but sometimes it happens by accident. After the Food and Drug Administration (FDA) banned thalidomide use in pregnant women, sales of the drug plummeted. In the 1990s, however, a group of patients with human immunodeficiency virus (HIV) started taking thalidomide to alleviate disabling symptoms. This unapproved use (called off-label use), which came about because consumers adapted the compound to their needs, eventually resulted in a new authorization for an old pharmaceutical and the creation of a new market. Celgene Corp. did not suggest this use for its drug Thalomid, but it did track it. The new market was an accident, but a very positive one for the patients and Celgene.

Building Involvement into Products

Customer involvement does not need to happen by chance, though. You can build it into your products. The right time to build customer involvement into your plans is when you are beginning to think about products for a new market. It starts by accepting a wider definition of the word *product*. To the new market, your product is more than the item or service that you deliver. Your product includes everything that your customers experience in their relationship with you, every contact with your customer. When your business advertises, sells, issues an invoice, handles complaints, and offers support, you are delivering your product.

Motorola's product is not cell phones and radios. It is Motorola. Palm Inc.'s product is not the handheld unit, the operating system, or the software. It is Palm's websites, its wireless network, its advertising. To a great extent, the product includes all the products of its licensees such as IBM, Handspring, Sony, Kyocera, and HandEra. When Sprint distributes a Kyocera phone with Palm's operating software and user interface, it represents Palm, Inc.. When Palm builds involvement into products, it has to include all these experiences as part of the product.

Companies can promote customer involvement but choose different strategies. Two strategies on how to design involvement into similar products are reflected in Siemens ICN and ROLM's former CBX product lines (see Figure 8-2).

Siemens ICN (Information and Communication Networks) makes central voice and data switches for telephone companies. These giant computerized systems sit in the core facilities for the

Figure 8-2. Mass versus individual tailoring and involvement—the vendor side.

SIEMENS' STRATEGY vs	ROLM'S STRATEGY
Provide telecommunications systems and solutions	Provide telecommunications systems and solutions
Large installations, costing millions of dollars	Smaller installations, costing hundreds of thousands of dollars
Tens of customers	Thousands of customers
Promote customer control of assets	Promote customer control of assets
Promote customer involvement	Promote customer involvement
One-on-one tailoring and involvement	Provide software for self-tailoring and involvement
Involvement designed in from beginning	Involvement designed in from beginning
Customers choose the features they want from a large menu	Customers choose the features they want from a large menu

*Siemens and ROLM both promoted customer involvement,
but with different strategies.*

large phone service suppliers such as U.S. West and Ameritech (part of SBC). In 2001, the company bought Efficient Networks, Inc., a company that makes the hardware and software that allow broadband connections to terminate in individual computers in offices and homes.

The management at Siemens ICN started with the intent of deciding where the various pieces of the companies should go.[1] It was clear from the beginning that the offering it was acquiring from Efficient Networks would not be a set of switches and modems. It would need to be a complete package that included engineering to tailor the products to individual telephone companies, support packages for those companies, special commercial terms and conditions, and even financing. The acquisition and the technology would be small parts of the overall product.

Siemens has an advantage in its market because it has only a few potential telecom customers to engage, so each customer can have input into how the product set (in the larger sense) works for them. The dollar values of each customer contract also support such individual attention, since the average customer spends millions of dollars per year with the company. Siemens's strategy is to work with each customer enthusiastically, teaming with the customer in the final configuration and operation of the system. A company with more customers or a smaller dollar value per customer would find it impractical to follow this strategy.

When the number of customers increases beyond your ability to provide individual support for each one, your strategy might be to design the product package so that the customers can do the tailoring for themselves. In a business similar to Siemens ICN's, ROLM Corp. used this strategy. Although ROLM no longer exists as a separate company (it was bought by IBM Corp. and then Siemens in the 1980s), it remains a good example of how to build a market by promoting customer involvement in a product.

In the 1970s, the choices in business phone systems (known as private branch exchanges, or PBXs) were sparse. You could get what the local phone company had or use a central office (CO) service and not have a PBX at all. In both cases, your business had very little choice in how the system worked or what it did for you. The systems were computer-based, but the company that owned or rented the system had little control over the computer.

ROLM produced a new kind of computer-driven system (the company named them Computerized Branch Exchanges, or

CBXs) that the customer could program to adapt the CBX to its own business. This was a significant shift of control to the owner of the CBX, and ROLM used the opportunities well.

With the CBX, the owner could conduct its own moves and changes. Instead of having to pay the local phone company (and wait days) each time someone wanted to move a desk in the office, the business could perform the move with a simple software command. The act is trivial, but the impact is important. With this change, businesses took control of their own phone systems. ROLM did not do the tailoring on an installation-by-installation basis. It created the opportunity for each of several thousand customers to tailor the installation of the system, almost on the fly.

The next step in allowing customer involvement was to tailor how the phone system made long-distance calls. Clearly, a computer could choose the best routing for each call, making it easier on people and less expensive for the business. However, effective software wasn't available to businesses until ROLM introduced route optimization software that the CBX owner could control. This innovation allowed the CBX owner to tailor the software, hardware, and calling patterns to match the needs of the business. Today it seems an obvious choice, but in the 1970s it was revolutionary.

Whereas Siemens ICN has relatively few but high-paying customers, ROLM had a scale issue. If the company were to succeed, it had to produce a product that cost much less (the typical sale was perhaps $100,000) and that it could sell to thousands of customers each year. So ROLM encouraged customers to do their own tailoring in every installation. By becoming involved in the way they configured the CBX, customers took more control of their telecommunications network. The more control customers had, the more likely they were to want to buy more

ROLM products. Self-determination was a part of the product that ROLM sold.

ROLM's package also included software, hardware, wiring, and engineering support. The product was not the CBX; it was much larger. ROLM worked to make it possible for the customer to tailor any and all of the components. Unlike Siemens with a small set of customers, the ongoing adaptation required almost no effort by ROLM. Customers could tailor their product at a low cost in the field.

No matter how tempting it is to lead with technology, ask your team to remember that the product is much, much larger. The larger product is what you can tailor, through involvement, to meet the needs of individual customers.

When to Start: A Management Choice

Tools that involve customers are less expensive to supply (in terms of time and people, as well as money) and easier to manage if you build them into the product from the beginning. As you define your market, you can position your product to be customer-involving.

The self-tailoring aspects of a product or service can also be added to other markets. For example, car manufacturers will sell a vehicle with sound and electronics systems designed to meet the market requirements of a broad segment of the car-buying public. The sound system offers minimal adaptability—perhaps you can add an equalizer. The assumption remains that the consumer chooses the car and then goes to aftermarket suppliers to tailor the electronics.

Today, however, we have the electronics and software capability to let the user participate in tailoring the car-driving experience. If a driver prefers to drink coffee and listen to the news in the morning and smoke and listen to soft jazz in the afternoon, why not adapt? There is no reason that a car could not tune into National Public Radio and shunt power to heat a coffee cup holder in the morning. It is not a far stretch of the imagination to ask a car to learn how long the driver takes to smoke a cigarette. With that information, the car could shunt cooled air to the cup holder for a soft drink, tune into an Internet jazz station, and open the ashtray at an appropriate time. If the driver listens to traffic reports, why not have the car learn that and then switch to the traffic reports at the correct time, returning to the jazz station after each report?

The ongoing adaptation would require little or no work by the car company. The manufacturer would program the car to tailor its functions to the user in the field. This scenario is not technologically innovative. The difference is a fundamental design decision to let the car tailor itself to the driver. Adding self-tailoring to products is not an engineering or marketing decision. It is a management choice.

Self-tailoring can also create knowledge for your business. If you give a television the ability to learn how its owners choose programs for future viewing, you can start to understand better how to market to those TV owners. A survey will give you some data, but is not as effective as measuring action. It would make sense, from a market development perspective, to offer a tool that helps users to view television, track the shows they have watched, and then learn from the observation. It would be even more useful if this tool could predict the shows that the user likes and record them without prompting, even if the user does not know that they are going to be on TV. That capability to learn and help the customer interact with the TV is the principle behind personal video recorders such as TiVo.

Focus groups or customer marketing cannot define in advance the experiences that such products create. Customers define them at their own pace. As that occurs, you can build in measurements and take action to let customers improve their own experience. It is a cyclical process, leading to ever-improving experiences. This process is highly iterative, and that's a benefit when you are trying to create and dominate a market. The faster you learn how people are using your product, the faster you can react to an opportunity, just as Celgene reacted to thalidomide being used off-label. That allows you to adapt to the new market and gives you a better chance of becoming the primary vendor.

What Products Can Self-Tailor?

One of the side effects of the miniaturization of electronics is that you can put a processor in almost any product that sells for more than a dollar. With the vastly reduced cost of chips and gates per chip, almost any product can add customer involvement at an almost trivial cost per unit for hardware.

If your product can use this processing power to become adaptive to users, it will have the opportunity to create its own markets and applications. Today, electronic pill bottles furnish research data to pharmaceutical manufacturers, but the potential is there to offer a product that will learn patients' needs and help them remember to take medicine. Dozens of VCRs are on the market, but until TiVo (or similar products sold under various labels), none began to use processing to learn users' habits and adapt to them. The concept is different from basic recording. The personal video recorder (PVR) involves and adapts to the customer. The positioning reflects that: The company's slogan is "TiVo, TV Your Way."

TiVo is aggressive in pushing involvement. Its press releases have claimed that it "was the first to deliver on the promise of consumer choice and control over TV viewing, building a loyal and passionate subscriber base." The latter part of that claim seems true. People who have bought and use TiVo (available in multiple configurations) appear to be intensely loyal to the idea of "TV Your Way." It is purely anecdotal, but I have yet to meet a user who is not pleased with the notion of having control over a medium that feels inherently uncontrollable to most people.

Once users get involved with a product, they get very inventive. They will find applications that you never considered. You can use this to your advantage. If people use Palm devices to unlock cars, they'll find other interesting applications that you did not consider for your new product. Unexpected uses for your product may help you increase sales or even create another new market.

To take advantage of that creativity, look at the low cost of computing power. Ask if you could use that power to make your product adaptive. Can you let your customers create the changes that they want and get instant gratification?

Well-designed customer involvement tools let the customer discover and develop new uses. LEGO's customers show the company many product innovations that will sell. When you build the experience-defining tools into your product, with or without electronics, those changes can avoid some field maintenance requirements. You need not dispatch support for changes if the customer makes the changes as she sees fit. For instance, when AOL users decide that they want to change their online channels, it costs AOL nothing. No staff members have to act; no one creates product requirement documents, AOL staff conducts no analysis, and the company expends no resources. The user changes the channels that he wants from the screen. Both the user and America Online benefit.

Don't Confuse Technology with Effect

Forgetting this rule may be easy, but the technology your business uses in your product is not what creates a new market. Worse, the technology can become a distraction and slow your effort to create and dominate a new market.

It is tempting to focus on the technology. Use of technical skill may be very attractive to your team and to the financial markets. It is rewarding for the team and highly interesting to those analysts and technical managers who follow the financial and trade markets.

However, many companies that have created and dominated new markets lead with non-cutting-edge, safe technologies. The digital cognoscenti consider AOL light years behind other services technologically. Yet, while OS2 may have been technically excellent, it flopped in the market as an operating system to replace Microsoft Windows. Early Palm products were far from cutting-edge computers, yet Palm created a new market with its products. Most LEGO products are small pieces of plastic and do not use technology at all. Each of these products, however, used innovative technologies to appear simple to users.

The lesson is not that dumbed-down products are better. The key point to remember is that simple and easy-to-use interfaces are often more important to users than technical elegance. When you invest your resources into sophistication you don't have them available to design ease of use. You are making a choice. The developers of the Apple Newton made choices to produce a great and sophisticated device, but the simpler Palm product line is the one that sells in the millions.

With limited time, people, and money, your choice is to invest in features you want the market to have, or to invest in features your customers will use each day. To build new markets, choose the latter.

The Moment of Truth: Installation

Jan Carlzon suggests the idea of "moments of truth."[2] These moments are not single events, but every instance in which your overall product touches the customer or potential customer. Carlzon, who ran a successful airline (SAS), noted that the moments of truth were not all on the plane. The obvious moment of truth is the flight, but moments also occur when the customer makes a reservation, changes planes, approaches a service counter, or even reads an advertisement. Carlzon's observation was that a business has innumerable moments of truth, and company employees have the responsibility to perform well at each one.

When you create a new market, one of the most critical moments of truth occurs before the customer gets full use of your product. Each product has a point when the user tries to start or install the product, to turn it on.

Many customers have grown to accept that installation or assembly will be arduous and painful. Recently I sat at a table with two naturalists and two business owners. We all worked on the same problem—setting the alarm on the watch that both scientists happened to own. After a half-hour, we were unable to do it. We are all reasonably intelligent, fairly creative folks. Yet a simple $50 watch baffled us. We were unable to become involved with a product designed for customer involvement.

Getting a benefit from the sophisticated alarm never became an issue, because the watch owners never got the alarm to work. This watch has tens of wonderful features that are unavailable to the owners. Someone spent the equivalent of several person-years and a small fortune putting the features in that watch and interface, but they are useless if the features cannot be used the first time.

I've also observed seven highly intelligent people assembling an underwater camera. It took almost three hours following the directions, and the camera did not work when they were done. In this case "did not work" means they could not get even one function to operate. They worked on it for several more hours, slept on it, and after several more attempts they found the problem on the second day. The new batteries were dead. Some cameras will alert the user to low battery power. This one did not.

Whether these seven people are incompetent is not, in the end, terribly important. Two issues will be critical to the future business of the product's maker, however. One is that the users may not enjoy the camera as much as they had hoped. The second is that users will give a tepid recommendation to their friends. They may have a little resentment (misplaced or not) toward the camera. Resentment such as this, when directed at your products, can cripple your work to create a new market.

Many users believe that they should be able to program a watch or VCR, and that it is not their fault that they cannot. If it is not a flaw in the user, is it a defect of the supplier? As Walter Mossberg, personal technology columnist for *The Wall Street Journal*, has often said, it is not the owner's fault that technology is so hard to use. Every time a user says the equivalent of "I'm computer challenged," that presents a problem for all computer makers. The shortcoming lies with the suppliers; the technology is not at fault. Instead, it is the way that technology is used by the supplier.

As an example, the sales of enterprise resource planning (ERP) software grew dramatically in the last decade. ERP software helps a business bring important parts of its business together (e.g., parts purchasing, inventory management, supplier interactions, orders tracking, financial management, and human resources functions). However, the vast majority of companies that could use ERP still do not have it. One reason is the failure rate of ERP installations. One survey found that well over half the CEOs of companies that had installed ERP regretted doing so. The same survey also identified that the failures were not the products. The problem, according to the executives surveyed, was how hard the software was to install correctly. Businesses spend a fortune to ensure that the interface for everyday use is easy. Some do not invest the same energy into the start-up process. It is a mistake that you should not repeat.

Smooth Installations: What You Can Learn About Your Products from a Wireless Network

Wouldn't it be nice if you could just walk into a room with a laptop computer and have it connected to other computers and the networks at blazing speeds, without wires? Any computer whiz can do it, but can you or I? The answer provides a lesson that may improve the products and services that you supply.

The Promise of Easy Installation: Did They Deliver?

Why would you want a wireless network? With all your PCs connected in your office or small business you can already share documents, software, or a high-speed Internet connection like T1 or DSL among all your users. You can download those big files in minutes instead of hours. Computer operations that only large companies could do before are now available to small businesses as well.

The attraction of wireless, though, is that you can plug a card into each computer, pop in a disk, and the network sets itself up. With no wires, you can move your laptop computer around the office and just log onto the Internet from where you are. It can run at speeds that are five or ten times faster than digital subscriber line (DSL) or cable modems. At home, you could work from bed or your kitchen and still surf the Net at high speed.

End-users will require easy and painless installations if these products are to create a new market among small businesses, especially since most small companies do not have IT staff and don't want to be their own IT experts. To open the small business market, the vendors must make the technology very easy to install.

We tried such an installation in our consulting firm. We learned a great deal. Our experience with three wireless office network products[3] appears typical of most networks and many other interesting technology products as well.

The most important lesson is that most managers and owners probably don't have enough time to install a wireless network. No matter how much you may want to save a few dollars, doing the installations yourself will eat up far more hours than you want. If you have a business to run, you can either invest your time into marketing, people, growth, or configuring computers. Configuring computers comes last.

The second lesson is that, even if you have the time, you may still need an IT department to install these networks. For example, we installed three products—Lucent's Orinoco product line, Proxim's Symphony, and Cisco Systems' Aironet—to avoid running cable. They were all inexpensive ($500 to $1,000 to connect four or five computers) and promised that anyone can install them.

In all cases, when we installed these products, the first thing that we needed was an expert to tell us what we needed. As you develop new products, such a requirement is not a problem if your customer has an expert on staff. If you are selling engines and you can count on technical support to exist at the customer site, you can provide a less intuitive solution. For line extensions, you can often assume that your customers know how to install familiar products. However, for new markets you should assume that your customers have no idea how to install and start your product. One key difference between America Online versus Prodigy and CompuServe in 1990s was that when AOL initiated its new market efforts, it strove for a "brainless" installation. You should do the same.

The publicity for the wireless networks implied such a simple installation. To get started, we called four distributors for one product. None could figure out how to configure our network and tell us what to buy. Overall, the technical support from the resellers caused more problems than they solved. In the end, one Proxim support person told us "Whomever you bought this from, you don't want to call them" for help. Tech support from the suppliers was much better, especially over the phone. A problem for suppliers, though, is that live technical support is a terribly expensive way to make installations work.

The Orinoco products, highly touted for ease of use, weren't. If your expertise is running a business, you probably do not know enough to install this product. The "wizards" just do not function for nontechnical folks. Worse, although we told them of our choice of DSL, the tech support team did not warn us that Orinoco is incompatible with AOL DSL (a common choice among small businesses). The installation never worked. Proxim's Symphony products installed much more smoothly, but not smoothly enough. Their instructions were admirable. Each manual showed every screen that might confuse a manager or owner. The product had enough smarts to do some of its own technical work, yet the installation ultimately failed. The Cisco network is up and running, the only one of the three product sets that succeeded in carrying data to all the computers we tried—without our having to use an IT consultant. However, to get it running required an engineer from Cisco and four hours of configuration, so installation still wasn't easy enough.

The Lessons for Your Business

The most important lesson to stress from this experience is that none of this difficulty comes from a lack of thinking about the problem by the supplier. Our firm deals with many of these providers. They are not trying to make the average user feel incompetent. They are producing what they truly believe are easy-to-use products. Each installation is designed to fit into a context of where and how the product will be used. If you assume the wrong context, your design will not work for your customers. What they don't realize is that what is easy to them is mind-numbing to the average business owner. Despite your best intentions, your firm may be doing exactly the same thing.

This has two serious effects. One is that good products don't sell well. People and businesses don't buy what they cannot use. The second effect is that you may stifle new markets because only technically adept people can participate.

What are the lessons for your business? Ask yourself, Are your own products and services any easier to use than these examples? How do you know? Just because you understand the products does not mean that the average business owner does. Don't assume that your business is easy for the user. Test it carefully.

This lesson doesn't just apply to technology products. It applies to watches, specialized clothing, games, new forms of sports drinks, even light bulbs. It's unreasonable to assume that customers will want to take an hour to figure out how to use a product that they have never seen before. You could be building resentment among the very customers you are trying to coalesce into a market. You could be losing references. Neither is a way to create and dominate new markets.

The User Perspective Drives Your Market

Success in creating markets often comes from making advanced technology invisible to the end-user. If the user has to invest time in learning how to tailor the product, it detracts from the experience of using it. The learning that LEGO engenders does not come from reading the instructions or learning how to use the blocks. It comes from letting each person use and adapt the blocks and software as she sees fit. In creating new markets, elegance in technology comes from how the user, not the designer, sees it. The user defines the experience, not the vendor.

This different emphasis (i.e., user over product) means that customers will play a different role in your growth. That role starts with letting customers define the experience that they get from your product. In this model, you don't generate a great product and let customers come to you. You generate a good product and let them adapt it. You design involvement into your product experience from the very beginning.

Something else happens when your business focuses on the customer experience. You divert the customer's attention from price to effect. If they like the effect, it can drive sales independently of price. This allows your margins to improve, and that can help fund your next new markets.

Designing user involvement into your products is not difficult. It can pay off in eliminating price resistance and making your product the one that everyone wants. After all, who wouldn't choose the option created just for you?

9

What Is the Role of Information Technology?

Reaching customers, automating processes, and allowing employees to do more with the same resources are all critical to growth. The normal role of the information technology (IT) department is to help solve these problems, but your technology team can also help make new markets work. However, the way to do this is not by creating electronic delivery and hoping for the best. Instead, the correct strategy is to use technology as a way to expand into markets that other parts of your company create. IT does not build markets, but in this chapter you will see where IT can play a role to help you to create new markets, dominate those new markets, and keep your company competitive in existing markets.

Note: Portions of this chapter originally appeared in "Should You Care What Keeps the CEO Up at Night?" *Business Communications Review* (June 2000), p. 70. Reprinted with permission.

Does Technology Create Markets?

As attractive as it may be to think that if you build it, they will come, the creation of a new technology does not systematically create new markets. Consider these two examples from Apple Computers, a company started by two guys who wanted to change the world from their garage. Steve Jobs once told his people that their role was to create an "insanely great" computer. His explanation to John Sculley, then president of Pepsi, was that the technology could change the world.[1] The result has been a series of interesting uses of technology and compelling products, such as the Apple IIe, the Macintosh, and the iMac.

As compelling as these products have been over time, none were actually new technologies. The newest part was the operating system for the Macintosh, which was an elegant and excellent implementation of existing software techniques. Apple's story is not a technology story, but the work of a company that has done a superb job of taking existing technologies, putting them together in great packages, and marketing them well.

The company has not always succeeded. The Apple Lisa computer was an interesting use of proven technologies that failed in the market.[2] Eventually, the best ideas from that computer became the core of the Macintosh. Perhaps the most spectacular example of an attempt by Apple to create a new market was the Newton, a handheld computer. Beyond the small size, a key innovation was that the company designed the system to recognize handwriting. That eliminated the need for every unit to have a keyboard.

When Apple created the Newton, it was an attempt to take new technology and create a market. This combination of a new handwriting recognition system with new electronics gave the handheld computer the ability to do much of what a full PC could do, without being tethered to a wall plug. The idea was, and still is, very attractive.

Yet the Newton was not a success at creating the market. Nor were other handheld products attempted by Psion, Casio, Hewlett-Packard, and IBM. The technology was there, but the market did not respond to it no matter how well the large companies applied marketing expertise. Technology did not create markets for Apple. In the end, Palm Computing created the market, using a better design.

Cable News Network (CNN) created a market that it continues to dominate. So did Music Television (MTV). Neither of these markets could have come into existence without the advanced technologies that allow AOL Time Warner and Viacom to broadcast them. Advanced technology enables the market and helps CNN and MTV to deliver programming, but by itself technology cannot create markets.

Technology is nonetheless key to helping you fill gaps in potential. Personal stereos came from excellent use of technology, starting with transistors. While AT&T's Bell Laboratories created transistors, it was other companies, such as Sony Corp., that created the markets by first finding a problem that needed solving and then applying existing technologies to solve them.

If you start with the technology, you may succeed in making a market. If you want to increase your chances of success, look at the problem and the potential gap that needs filling. Then look for technologies to fill that gap.

Making the Process Repeatable

Can a company repeatedly make new markets with proven technologies? Sony has, General Electric has, and Polaroid has. Most companies have not. It isn't all a matter of chance. The key to making success repeatable is applying technology well. The difference between Bell Laboratories and Sony is not just the culture of the parent business or country. There is a similar distinction between Lockheed Martin Corp. and the Skunkworks developed inside Lockheed. The key difference is the conscious decision to apply technology to specific problems.

Of course, identifying problems in the military is easier than in business-to-business or consumer markets. Still, the process is the same. What the management at Lockheed Martin did was to identify the critical problems first, then marshal the resources and technologies to develop a plane that would solve the problems. The Skunkworks was a team that focused on the problem and applied the technology.

Sony's success in consumer electronics is not a legend of innovative technologies looking for a problem to solve, but the reverse. The Sony Walkman worked because executives at the company identified a gap between what consumers could have and what they wanted. That potential became a market when Sony produced the technology, product, and marketing to fill the gap with a personal stereo.

Sony, Palm, Lockheed, and CNN all identified the potential between the problem and the solution and then used technologies to fill that gap. The key to successfully creating markets with technology involves this simple principle: The successful company starts with the potential and applies the appropriate technology, not vice versa.

Which Technologies Should You Apply?

When you start trying to create markets with technology, you are theoretically unlimited by any restrictions on which technologies to apply. However, the real world doesn't work that way.

Even though you may try to avoid it, the team of people that you work with will usually be limited to the technologies that are top of mind. The effect is similar to having blinders on. Be careful to make sure that your people look past recent technological innovations to the problem that your customers are trying to solve. Otherwise, they face a crippling limitation to new markets.

Many business owners use the word *technology* as synonymous with the Internet and faster computer processing. Thousands of businesses have defined success at using technology as being online and having newer, faster computers. The result has often been worse than wasted money. It has often been wasted opportunity. The money spent on developing a Web presence is not critical. The attention your best minds invest to get the business web-ready is irretrievable. Often you would do better to invest that attention in creating new markets.

Wal-Mart is an excellent example. Two winters in a row, the nation's fastest-growing retailer shut down its website as it entered the Christmas season, the most profitable period of the year. Wal-Mart chose to invest instead in the work and other forms of technology that helped it expand retail locations and get more merchandise to shelves.

Technologies that help drilling and construction companies, traditional retailers, plastics companies, biochemical firms, gas stations, and private schools to grow may not be as appealing as the Internet. Attractive or not, they are just as important to new markets. If you allow your people to restrict themselves with a sole focus on the Internet, you will be running full speed with blinders on.

How do you choose technologies in which to invest? You can take three approaches toward technologies for creating new markets. Your choices are to pick:

1. The newest, most popular technologies

2. Technologies that are comfortable

3. Technologies that help you fill gaps

Choosing the Newest, Most Popular Technologies

If you are most concerned with gaining funding and support, you will find that working with trendy technologies will help. People love to invest in the next great thing, whether that new toy works or not.

Choosing the hot trend is a trade-off. You are exchanging the chances of future success at new markets for the funding and support to get through today. Whether you run a separate business or a division of a larger company, you may find that when the trend changes, you get left behind. For example, Webvan got substantial support early in the dot-com boom cycle, yet by the beginning of 2001, the company was unable to get enough funding to maintain full operations. The trends had moved on, but the company had not. Being a dot-com in 2001 and 2002 is not an attractive way to gain support from venture capitalists and larger companies. Hot trends, almost by definition, cool quickly.

The other reason to choose a new and popular technology is for a function that it promises. Frequently, the new and unproven technology may be the best choice for what you want to do, but that's not always the case. The risk is that your team will fall in love with the technology, irrespective of whether it's the right choice.

When you decide to start with the hot technologies to attract support, your best point of reference may be the popular and trade daily press. Traditional and new periodicals such as *The Wall Street Journal, Wired, Fast Company,* and *BusinessWeek* can all point you to the latest hot technology.

Choosing Comfortable Technologies

You will find an inherent conflict between comfort and creating and dominating new markets. Technologies that are comfortable bring two attributes to your new market effort. One is that they can be of real use. AOL used proven technologies to help create its market. Sony has taken advantage of proven technologies to build exceptional products. Your business can also reduce the risk of failure by using comfortable technologies as tools to create markets. Comfortable technologies reduce the risk to your plan. Known technologies allow you to save time and money by using what you know. They also help you avoid overbuilding a product just because you have new technology that can do things the old technology could not. You can make life easier on your team if you direct their efforts to the more comfortable focus of known processes and markets.

Comfortable technologies also bring a second, contrary, attribute. For many people, the strongest reason to avoid creating new markets is comfort. New is uncomfortable, new markets even more so. Many of your people may choose to focus on comfortable technologies, not because they are the correct choice, but simply because they are safe. This creates the risk of missing great new technologies. However, the greater risk is in taking that attitude all the way into the new market effort itself. Then your entire new market effort is at risk from a desire for comfort. New markets are inherently uncomfortable, nervous places to be. If your team needs to be comfortable in all areas, the new market may be more challenge than it can take.

If you can manage the balance of comfort and risk, known technologies can give you real advantages in conserving time and money. In this option, your starting point for choosing technologies is the familiar technologies that your team already knows how to use to your business' best advantage.

Choosing the Technologies That Can Help You Fill Gaps

The best process to create and dominate new markets is to focus on gaps between a strong need and a solution. Starting with this third option will give you a greater chance to open a new market. It also ignores technology in favor of a focus on problems. Your starting point is gaps and problems. In this model, identifying the gap that customers will pay to fix comes before choosing a technology to fix the gap.

The risk is that no technology will exist to solve the problem. If so, your new market effort will fail. To manage that risk, you need your team to survey all technologies, whether you know them or they are yet unproven. You may need to create a technology, and that carries its own risks.

Technologies, Gaps, and the Unknown

The problem to solve is not finding the right technology. The problem is finding the gap in potential between what the prospective customers have and what they badly need. The caveat to consider is that you run some risk of misunderstanding that gap. However, new gaps are forgiving. When you are focusing on a new market, you have the leeway to make mistakes and corrections. You must be ready to react quickly to correct mistakes.

A company that can correct course well is Cisco Systems. One tenet of Cisco's product development cycle is that getting a good product to market in ninety days is better than getting a perfect product to market in a year. A former managing director at Cisco talks about the company's "ruthless execution." In this precept, if a project cannot be done in ninety days, it does not get resources. The reason long projects fail in new markets is that your understanding of the market is almost always a little off. It's tempting to perfect your product with market research before you release it, but new markets are very difficult to study. The longer you take to get to customers, the further off you are likely to get. The best way to understand your new customers may be to initiate the market, then quickly work with your customers to improve the product.

If a product is more than the hardware or software, it becomes less technology dependent and more design and services oriented. The product is not just the deliverable for which you collect money; the product is everything that touches the customer, including the bill itself. As you widen your view of what a product is, you reduce the impact of technology on that product. Amazon.com is not just a website; the company is a massive system to collect books and other products, pay for them, offer them, bill for them, and then find, pack, and ship them. The company's sophisticated web technologies are only a small part of the product. If you will, the product is convenience. Technology is an important delivery mechanism, but only that.

Amazon.com has patented some critical technology, but you do not need unique technology to succeed. Often, several companies have access to the same technology, but only one will succeed at creating and dominating the market. Palm Computing was not the first company to use common technologies to build a personal digital assistant (PDA), but it was the company that ultimately created and defined the market. Despite three attempts by Microsoft to challenge the market leader, the Palm platform continues to dominate. Technology plays a small part in the dominance. Palm, Handspring, HandEra, and Sony all use different hardware platforms and, except for the operating system, third parties provide most of the software. What is unique to Palm's family of products is the packaging of interface and services. The Palm products, compared with Microsoft-based palm products, are simple to use, stable, have good battery life (which is nontrivial to the users), and install software (and a wide selection of software) easily. Technologies contribute to each of these attributes, but how they are chosen and then presented to the user are what makes the difference. Palm's founders intentionally chose these interfaces because they concluded that the gap was in usability, not computing. When you choose to develop a product that uses new technologies, remember that to the customer, the technology is only part of the solution. The product consists of much more than the object that people hold in their hand; it includes all of the ways that your customer works with the product (see Figure 9-1).

The way to look at a product is the way that Jan Carlzon did when he identified every point of customer contact as a moment of truth. A product helps you create and dominate a market when you ensure that all the moments of truth contribute to filling the gap for the customer.

Figure 9-1. What makes a product?

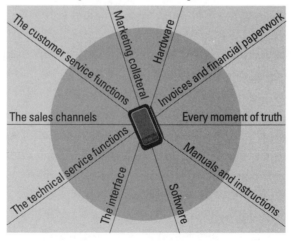

*To the customer, the technology
is only part of the solution.
All these are parts as well.*

In the end, buying and creating technology is a very expensive way to buy and create a toolbox. You always have the option of buying fancy systems because they look great, but you are better off buying boring tools that get your job done.

Aligning Technology Development Teams with New Markets

At Cisco Systems, the focus on understanding customers and gaps has led to an interesting phenomenon. Cisco's internal IT departments have also acted as part one of the company's product development team. If you've installed the Cisco Aironet wireless network (see Chapter 8), the installation wizards that you used were developed, written, and put on disk by an IT staffer at Cisco. The principle is simple: IT staffers understand the problems best, and often they are the right people to use the appropriate technology to fill those gaps. In an unusual way, Cisco is aligning technology development teams with the market.

Whether you choose Cisco's model of letting IT develop products or a more traditional role of having product teams (or a mix) do the work, you have a basic conundrum. Both product developers and IT teams are vulnerable in two ways:

▶*They focus on their own solution to the problem.* It can be very tempting for a product or IT specialist to put the product before the need for that product. Unfortunately, the result may be products that are solutions in search of a problem to solve.

▶*They focus on the market as they understand it.* This usually means the market as it exists today. If your objective is to extend the product line, this focus may work well for you. If you want to create and dominate new markets, these perspectives are counterproductive.

So how do you get your teams to focus on new markets? This responsibility belongs to general managers and owners. Your task is to help the product development and IT teams to add a new perspective: to focus on the gap that defines the potential new market.

The new focus is a change for most IT managers. Traditionally, most IT attention goes to critical issues such as:

"Is my network stable?"

"How far can I cut costs without hurting users?"

"Is this the right technology for the foreseeable future?"

Although these are important questions, they don't build markets. They also aren't top concerns for most company presidents. What are their top concerns? The answers to that question may not be what your teams expect, but they apply directly to getting executive support for great projects. To gain backing from corporate presidents, let's look at what keeps them counting sheep.

As noted in Chapter 3, when we've interviewed executives who run companies in the United States, Europe, and Asia and asked them to tell us their biggest problems, the same two have come up consistently. These are the issues that get corporate attention and funding:

1. Creating and dominating new markets

2. Getting and keeping the right people

Other concerns are important, just not important enough. Executives have more things on their desk than they have time to address them. They take the issues in order of importance and apply resources to them in the same way. If your team wants time, people, or money for a technology project, it has a better chance to get those resources if that project deals with one of these top concerns instead of the tenth. The question is whether the project is, or could be, at the top of the list for the company.

Most of the management trends of the past decade are not on the list of top concerns. According to surveys done by The Meyer Group, issues that other people find critical typically do not rate that way with CEOs. Here are some examples:

Hot Topics That Don't Keep CEOs Awake

Vision and leadership

Network uptime

Mergers and acquisitions

Time to market

Cost cutting

Quality

Risk reduction

Customer service

Empowerment

Reengineering

Installation of enterprise resource planning software

These are issues that IT staffs have identified as important but don't rise to the top of the list of CEO concerns—unless they directly affect creating new markets and getting and keeping people.

CEO Concern 1: Creating and Dominating New Markets

The axiom is that the first company to define a market has the best chance of dominating it. Executives are focused on doing exactly that. They put great emphasis on trying to define a future market through the company's own vision and technologies. This may seem the purview of the marketing departments, but company presidents often feel the need to focus on it personally.

A systems company president hoped to use dominance in one market to define the market in another. "The idea," he said, "is to get the wireless providers to follow the standards adopted by the wireline companies." These happen to be technology standards that were partially set by this supplier. If the company can get new companies to define their needs in line with these norms, this supplier "can use one architecture to grow the business." By defining the standards for a new market, this company would be the first and dominant supplier in that market. This outcome, in the president's view, was too important to delegate.

Many executives talk of trying to set the rules of competition for a new market, because setting those rules could make it easier to establish dominance. The president of a network products company said his priority was defining the ground rules for a new set of technologies. "Can we capture the high ground and mind share of the buying community?" The head of a growing service provider wanted to set the standards for the "governance and use of web control, [and] the smart use of technology to do that."

Each individual market has different ground rules. What one set of customers absolutely needs, another will not value. That creates unique problems when a company wishes to develop new markets. Reliability is a good example. Getting extreme reliability is not critical for most customers. If a supplier of Internet browsers ships an early version that's only 90 percent reliable, users either adapt and accept or delay installing the product. However, customers of telephone and data communications products won't accept anything less than 100 percent reliability.

Mature products are often more reliable, but new markets don't wait for hardware and software to mature. Several CEOs surveyed were trying to walk this tightrope of determining exactly how much reliability to have before entering the market. One executive worried over the comparative values of "being first to get to [and define a] market, against waiting to be highly reliable. How do you balance those?"

The common lore is that senior management is very focused on ways to cut costs. However, none of the executives surveyed had cost control on their lists. Dollars and risk are different issues.

One top Asian CEO worried more about missing the growth opportunity than about costs: "We are entering a new world. Absorbing new information is a problem. Do we really know [the market]?" This executive focused on "industry and technology trends to help guide headquarter's directions." Instead of trying to imprint the market with his company's technologies, he wanted to "keep our eyes and ears open and not miss important trends. . . . [W]e have new products, but the market is not ready yet." For this CEO, as with almost every other executive, opportunity costs outweigh operating costs. IT investments are viewed in terms of opportunity costs, not cash outlays.

CEO Concern 2: Finding and Keeping People

The CEO of a quickly growing manufacturer said, "First has to be keeping great people and then attracting more of them." Most other CEOs put something similar in first or second position on their list of concerns.

According to the chief operating officer of one dominant supplier, "The thing that limits our ability to grow is finding and keeping people." Software people were so important to his firm that the company moved key software from a proprietary software platform to one that prospective employees would find attractive. Changing that software code was a risky and expensive change, one that customers had not requested. If something went wrong, it would threaten the company's ability to deliver new products. Why, then, would the COO demand it? Two reasons overrode the risks: One was the company's desire to enter a new market and the other was to improve the company's ability to recruit and retain good people.

CEOs do get concerned with recruiting and benefits, but those are not the issues that preoccupy them; they have other people to deal with those concerns. The value these CEOs strive to add is to make the work attractive and interesting. Getting good people to come and stay is a quality of work life issue as much as a benefits issue. The CEOs interviewed made a point of involving themselves in looking for ways to increase satisfaction on the job, knowing it can attract and hold the people who can help build markets. IT tools for productivity are important, but not compared with this.

IT as a Tool for New Markets

Neither of the top concerns of CEOs is a technology problem, but they use technology as part of the solution. When a company changes core software, it involves technology. The question of product reliability versus speed to market involves technology. What is important is that technology, in each case, is a tool to reach a larger issue. Proposing technology is not the correct answer. Proposing a solution to the problem will get the attention of the CEO.

IT can clearly help extend dominance in existing markets.

Information technology can also be a useful tool when you work to improve the quality of the workplace experience. The question is whether IT can help your business create and dominate new markets. In two cases, the answer is yes. IT can be a tool for new market creation when a company is:

▶Expanding geographically

▶Identifying new customer sets and markets within existing companies

Geographic Expansion

In general, hospitals are not growing rapidly. One exception is Woman's Hospital in Baton Rouge, Louisiana. Growth for the hospital and the services it provides could come as a result of the female population increasing, or the institution could decide to grow into other parts of the state. Despite the difficulty of pioneering advanced network technologies, the hospital is using them to grow into new geographic markets across the state. CEO Teri Fontenot says that she does not want to grow by supplanting local healthcare facilities. Instead, she wants to help all healthcare facilities be better. The IT department at Woman's Hospital is a key to growing into those new markets.

Many hospitals have used technology to increase access to the patient base or to reduce the cost of service, but Woman's Hospital is going well beyond that. Fontenot explained: "We are upgrading our fetal monitoring system" with a new technology that looks for aberrations in heart tones during labor and alerts the nurse to call the physician. "We want to provide capability remotely [that] brings sophisticated services to remote areas. It keeps smaller facilities from having to buy expensive equipment. [Even with that equipment] they might not have the physician on staff to help interpret results. The things we take to other areas are specialties that smaller hospitals are not set up to support. It's good for the hospitals, good for the clinicians, good for the patients."[3] This application of technology gives Woman's Hospital access to a new market.

Woman's Hospital is at the leading edge of some new technologies, trying to deliver crisp images across dedicated wide area networks consistently and securely. Although the technology team finds high-speed, high-resolution imaging interesting, Fontenot does not. Her eyes light up when she talks about the effect IT is able to deliver or enable in new markets. The technology allows Woman's Hospital to "have maternal fetal medical specialists on staff [who can] go out to remote areas through telemedicine." This capability attracts new physicians. Physicians "want their patients to get good nursing care. They want their visits to the hospital to provide convenience [and] be hassle free. That is worth more to them than money." The information technology team helps them do both.

Fetal monitoring is just one application. To serve the new markets better, Woman's Hospital plans to use advanced technologies to provide ultrasound and chest X-ray services as well as digital signatures and digital charts to patients across the state. All these capabilities will make work easier for the doctors, too, and that will bring more opportunity to the hospital. IT helps the hospital to attract new doctors in remote areas. New doctors bring patients and "that's the carrot for us." As Woman's Hospital grows into a new market, IT is key to the effort.

New Markets Inside the Same Companies

As the market leader in an existing market, Cisco Systems has limited room for growth in the IT budgets of its traditional corporate customers. Cisco now takes eight of every ten sales, and it clearly cannot ever get ten of ten. Where does the company look for growth opportunities?

One answer is new markets. Cisco funds new market work outside its normal, very technical customer set. Recognizing that IT managers are going to buy Cisco products as fast as their business grows, Cisco management started to wonder how it could help these customers grow faster. It chose to fuel more demand by reaching beyond the IT market to the general business managers of corporations.

CEOs and CFOs are a new market for Cisco, and they are a market that has not cared to become involved in what Cisco is known for, plumbing for the Internet. The key to providing value to that new market came from the IT team.

Karen Brunett, a Cisco marketing director, explains that the company realized that it had internal applications that demonstrated something besides plumbing. "Applications like customer care, Internet commerce, and supply chain management are designed to be attractive to functional management."[4] CEOs and CFOs who do not care about data transmission do care about using these tools to open new markets.

Cisco's IT teams developed these applications for a real-world customer, Cisco. When proven, Brunett's team offers them as templates or reference architectures for customers. These implementations will not work for every company, and Cisco is not concerned with selling off-the-shelf applications. "IT created an application called Metro. It allows us to do all our expense reports online. What we did was to take this [application] to customers to show what could be done. Meanwhile a start-up company has created an application that is even better, and we partner with them." The key to Cisco is not the sale of the application, but that functional management in a company will start to use intelligent network applications. No matter who modifies the application, Cisco usually supplies the network products.

The company uses fairly sophisticated technologies, but the prospective customers won't see them. For Cisco, the friendlier and easier that each application appears, the more attractive it will be for the prospective customers. That will lead to more usage, and more need for Cisco's core products. This concept also applies at Woman's Hospital. The more technological magic the hospital's IT team displays in its tools, the less the doctors want to use them.

In both of these cases, IT develops tools that help companies enter new markets that would otherwise be unavailable. And in the end, customers will measure the development teams' skill in their ability to make the technology effective but invisible. What makes the market effort work is the effect, and the less the user sees of how you make that effect, the better.

10

Using Credibility in Creating and Dominating Markets

Once you have chosen to create a market, you must confront a difficult question: How do you enter the market so that it grows rapidly but leaves your business in a dominant position? Your new market effort must be based on believable and convincing ideas and people to attract potential customers. Credibility is always defined by the buyers or their advisers. How much credibility is enough? Your business can never have too much.

There are numerous ways to add credibility to your new market effort. Some are less obvious, or even counterintuitive. Four of the latter are discussed in this chapter. These options include:

►Viral marketing

►Careful selection (and rejection) of your customers and investors

201

►Production trials

►Using competition

Viral Marketing

When you wish to conserve your resources, an ideal marketing plan requires little cost, leverages flexibility, replicates itself with no effort by the sponsor, and works automatically. Viral marketing does that. The technique is to create something so attractive that people not only want to have it, they want others to have the same product as well. To many users, the most credibility you can get comes from other users. The users become the sales force, and sometimes the users will be your distribution vehicles as well. Napster file-sharing software and fax machines are examples of successful viral marketing efforts.

Napster Inc. started as a file-sharing "community" in 1999. To use the service, you load software that allows you to search the media and music files on the computers of any other Napster users. The same software allows you to share with any or all other Napster users.

If only two people had Napster, it would be fairly useless. However, if you got all of your friends to load the software, you would have access to all the unrestricted media files on their computers. The more users you got, the more media files you could find and copy for your own use. As Napster's user base grew, the users became the sales force and distribution vehicles for the software. If you wanted to know what music was available to download from a friend, you would use Napster software to find it. To get music from that or another friend, you would use Napster software. Communication between two users was done through the software. To be useful, everyone in the community had to have a copy. So people who wanted music started to ask their friends to get Napster software, which in 2001 was free to the end-user. Those friends asked more friends, and it multiplied in the same way that a virus spreads from host to host. This file sharing may be illegal, but because of the viral way in which file-sharing programs spread, it is proving difficult to stop the many alternatives to Napster that have propagated.

For viral marketing to succeed, you need:

▶A very attractive product

▶Many people using that product

▶The perception of a reasonable price and easy access

There are some myths about viral marketing which, if you subscribe to them, can inhibit your success. For example:

▶The product doesn't need to be a consumer product.

▶The product or service doesn't need to be distributed using the Internet.

▶The product or service doesn't need to be free.

An example is fax machines. One fax machine is not very useful, but if you can get your customers, vendors, and partners to each get a machine, all the devices become more useful because they can communicate with each other. If the function (not the device) is attractive, they begin to sell each other. Early in the history of fax machines, it is possible that users pestering other users sold more products than the marketing programs. When users talk other people into getting your product, you are replicating sales through viral marketing.

Some products have worked as viral products, and some have not. Word of mouth is what causes a product to be acquired. User-to-user recommendations also create the credibility that can help you to establish a new market. Here are some examples of hits and misses with the viral marketing technique:

Successes	Failures
AOL Instant Messenger	MSN's Messenger
Fax machines	Free Internet telephone service
Napster-style file sharing (e.g., Gnutella)	
E-mail	

A word of caution: You may lose control of your marketing effort when you create a virus. If you release a product that you wish to retrieve, you may find it difficult to get that product back. Consider Gnutella as an example. Unlike Napster, Gnutella software allows file sharing without a central computer, so users can trade files without going through servers run by a separate company. Napster as a company offers some control over its servers that store shared files. In 2000, when Napster shut down completely, the file trading stopped because it all ran through Napster's central computers. Gnutella's lack of a central computer means there is no single place to halt the file trading.

File sharing now poses a particular problem for America Online. The original Gnutella product was a beta software package created by two people who work for AOL.[1] They posted it on the Internet in March 2000. AOL took it off the network that day, but during that short window, many people found Gnutella and distributed the software and started to improve the package. Through the acquisition of Time Warner, AOL now owns large numbers of records and books, most of which the company prefers to sell for money and protect under copyright laws. Gnutella and other decentralized file-sharing programs like it make it possible to share music and books for free, and in a way that no number of lawsuits or court orders could control. In other words, it will potentially make AOL's music investments worthless.

Programmers have distributed millions of copies of improved Gnutella clones, and no matter how much AOL might like to stop the distribution, it is too late. Once you start viral marketing, the genie is out of the bottle and will not go back no matter what you or the courts try to do. The effort to contain an out-of-control viral marketing plan can siphon time, people, and money from your new market.

Choosing the Right Customers and Investors

Regis McKenna, the technology marketing consultant, has often pointed out that your first customers are not just important for their revenue value. Their presence on your customer list makes a statement about you and the market that you are creating. That assertion can increase or decrease the credibility of you and the market. You will find it easier to collect early sales if you can show off customers that your prospective users perceive as leaders. Since different groups of customers have different ideas of whom the leaders are, a challenge is making sure that you understand the perceptions of your key audience. The risk is that different groups have very different perceptions.

Different Customers, Different Perceptions
Centric Software, Inc. has been creating a market for collaborative manufacturing and supply software. This product has been useful to automobile and airframe manufacturers, who use it to get synergy from numerous suppliers and their own design

teams. Centric's initial customer set includes Volvo, BMW, and ITT Automotive. The list also includes United Airlines, Swissair, Continental Airlines, Inc., and KLM Royal Dutch Airlines. These customers like to buy from vendors who sell to companies that they respect. For Centric and for you, the choice of customers positions the vendor. Rightly or wrongly, the automotive industry places a different level of credibility on the name Volvo than it does on Hyundai. Members of the airline industry are more comfortable following the lead of United Airlines than the lead of a regional or third-world carrier.

Centric would also like to create a market among high-technology manufacturing companies, such as Palm, Inc., OmniSky Corp., and Juniper Networks, Inc. Having Volvo as a customer is an asset when selling to General Motors/Saab, but this is a different audience. The problem is not lack of need. Palm and OmniSky both have strong uses for this kind of product. OmniSky (which provides wireless modems and service for users of personal digital assistants) makes extensive use of partners who manufacture its modems, own and maintain the wireless network that OmniSky service uses, and supply technical support. Collaboration is not something nice to have, it is key to the business. With intelligent sharing of ideas and designs, OmniSky can speed new products to market acceptance. It can also avoid redesigning products. Using collaborative software as a tool for sharing ideas can help keep competitors from gaining a presence in that market. Avoidance of needless redesign costs can make the difference between profit and loss.

Palm's current market dominance in personal digital assistants (PDAs) is dependent on how well it can deliver total solutions to its customers. Those solutions are no longer single vendor, single product efforts. Palm also partners with service providers, software companies, licensees, and resellers of its products. Palm has to be able to support integration of the products of many companies in order to hold on to its market share dominance. Collaboration among partners is not an option, it is a requirement.

When Palm and OmniSky look at suppliers for critical processes, they need to feel comfort that the vendors understand them and their businesses. To many high-technology executives, an automotive company is not a great example. Technology companies view automotive companies as slow, bureaucratic, inflexible, and unresponsive, traits that no modern technology company wishes to emulate. Using a car company as an example is not likely to create comfort for prospective technology clients and might even be a distraction when selling to Palm.

The Importance of Choosing First Customers with Care

If you choose to sell to the first customer that your sales team or channel presents you in a new market, you are defining your image to any future customers in that market. If you choose to sell to a company that prospective customers will perceive as a second-tier player, those prospective customers may see you as a second-tier player as well. If you sell to the premier customer(s) in a market, you are more likely to define yourself as a premier company. Choose your first customers with care.

That said, you have a risk here as well. If you are too choosy, you can wind up with no references or revenue when you need them. This is especially likely if you choose to define the product around the requirements that you and your team set, instead of the requirements that your customers define.

In the 1970s, a company named Mardix (which has changed ownership since these events occurred and were shared with the author) was becoming dominant in the market for physical access control products among customers who needed to control building access. Offering a better solution than card access provided, Mardix started to create a market in high-end access control systems.

Early customers defined the company's position as well as the market. Los Alamos Scientific Laboratories, Sandia National Laboratories, Northrop Corp., General Dynamics Corp.'s airframe facility, and GTE Defense were all early customers. Each of these customers took comfort from the fact that the others were buying. This led to multiple sales to government contractors.

Sales at General Dynamics and Northrop made it easier to sell to the airplane manufacturing operations at McDonnell Douglas and Lockheed Martin as they were working on the DC-10 and L-1011, respectively. As important as McDonnell and Lockheed were, they were both much less successful in planes than The Boeing Co., so Mardix went to Boeing next.

Boeing said no. The arguments for savings, efficiency, and security were not an issue for Boeing. The operating manager with the authority to decide simply said, "If McDonnell and Lockheed are doing it, we won't. We built a more successful operation by doing things our way."

The result was an impasse. Mardix had a product that was succeeding across the defense industry and in the smaller airframe companies, yet the world's leading airframe manufacturer refused to follow. A sale to Boeing first would have changed how the rest of the airframe industry looked at Mardix. Although Mardix was highly successful in several industries, by accepting those first customers in the airframe business, Mardix accidentally defined itself as second tier.

For market-leading customers, involvement can be just as reassuring as following the leader is for other companies. In Boeing's case, Mardix wound up tailoring the products to match specifications suggested by the Boeing managers, building a special version just for Boeing. Both companies were pleased with the results, and Mardix was able to market to the rest of the commercial aerospace industry with the reassuring image of having Lockheed, McDonnell, and Boeing as customers. The lesson is to be careful to whom you sell. It will affect whom you can sell to after that.

Letting the People with the Problem Add Credibility to Your Solution

The same is true for taking money. Just as customers can define your image to other prospective customers, so can investors. A new customer wants to know that you are for real and that its investment in your business will last. Investments by other firms can help reassure the customer. Credibility comes from people who invest money for products; it also comes from people who invest money for the future.

The reverse is a possible loss of credibility, which can put the entire market at risk, not just your company. If you appear to be supported by risky companies, prospective customers may view your ideas and your business as a risk.

Juniper Networks, of Sunnyvale, California, was successful in avoiding those risks. The company was founded in 1996 to solve an Internet speed problem. Scott Kriens, the CEO, said: "As the Internet grows, it reaches a scale never before [experienced]." This scale dwarfs the ability of then-current technologies to support the Net. If the Internet outgrows the technologies, it will slow and could start to lose the data it sends. Unless someone solves the problem, all the companies who need the Internet to prosper are at risk. Kriens says, "New architecture and technology from large-scale computing must be brought to networking. We think this actually creates a new industry, building the network equivalent of supercomputers."[2] This led to the development of a series of extremely high speed network routing systems, consisting of both hardware and software, that would support levels of Internet traffic not considered remotely possible even a few years earlier. As *The Wall Street Journal* noted in 1997, "The technology is considered essential to ending bottlenecks on the Internet." [3]

Kriens and the Juniper team carried a substantial level of personal credibility, but you can always use more. Juniper had a product that, on paper, looked superb. However, so did a dozen other companies, some of which had years of commercial experience and strong track records. As Juniper was preparing to ship products in 1997, *The Wall Street Journal* specifically noted the company by saying, "Start-ups in the data networking area always face long odds, because of the expense of developing such complex products, the level of competition, and the presence of Cisco Systems, Inc., which is trying to squeeze out challengers by offering an end-to-end line of products." [4]

The primary customers of these products were companies that were betting their business on their own ability to carry much more data. "Vinton Cerf, widely regarded as the 'Father of the Internet,' and senior vice president for Internet engineering at MCI Communications Corp., [says] to keep up with traffic, 'we are going to require speeds of 2.4 gigabits [a quadrupling of capacity] between our nodes by next year.' "[5] These potential customers did not have the luxury of making a mistake on a young and unproven firm like Juniper.

From the customer's perspective, a great product is only a small percentage of the risk. If a company has a great product but can't manufacture it in a consistently reliable manner, the product fails. If the company can't support the product when the customer installs it, the product is a washout for customers. If the company's management is not strong enough to keep the company viable for many years, the product is not successful. Even if it is only the company's investors that are weak, customers may be unwilling to risk investments in great technology.

Smart customers consider all of these attributes to be part of the "product" that they buy (see Figure 10-1).

Kriens knew that he should choose his investors carefully. Juniper's first investments came from "top-drawer venture capitalists like Kleiner, Perkins, Caulfield & Byers; New Enterprise Associates; Benchmark Capital; Crosspoint Venture Partners; and Institutional Venture Partners."[6] Those were names that gave the Juniper team immense credibility among its prospective clients, but Kriens went a step further. "We were very fortunate to have a hard problem, that was very important to a lot of people, and [in which] there was not a great deal of high-quality work being done."[7] Kriens invited the people with the problem to invest in the solution. This investment was not to buy product, but to buy access to, and help ensure, the future. "The primary driver behind the motivation of investors in Juniper's early days was the combination of highly regarded talent assembled in an area where talent was known to be generally scarce, and alterna-

Figure 10-1. Attributes of the "product" that customers are looking for when they buy.

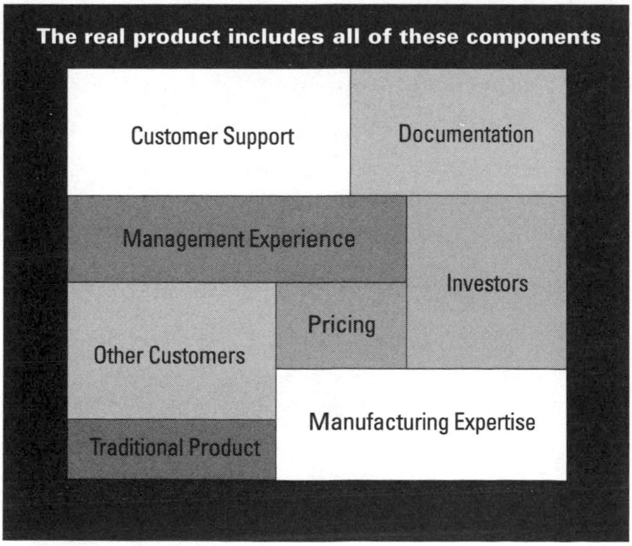

The real product includes all of these components

Customer Support

Documentation

Management Experience

Investors

Other Customers

Pricing

Manufacturing Expertise

Traditional Product

tives were few. . . . It also became a self-fulfilling dynamic, as investors were [told] who the other investors were. It was too easy and too cheap for them to participate versus the alternative of being left out of whatever the others saw [as an opportunity]." [8]

When four of the world's largest telecommunications equipment makers all agree to fund a product, it sends a message. There are very few places where Telefon AB LM Ericsson, Nortel Networks, Lucent Technologies, the (then) Siemens/Newbridge Networks venture, 3Com Corp., and WorldCom Inc.'s UUNET all come together. These investors went a long way to making Juniper a comfortable choice for Internet service providers.

With a combination of a highly credible product, company, and team, Juniper went on to capture a commanding share of the market. It is unlikely that the company could have been so successful without the credibility from those investors and early customers. If you wish to do as well, be careful how you choose yours.

Production Trials

An unexpected problem with some of Centric Software's first customers was that they would buy the software but not actually put it into production use. When you choose your prospective customers, you may find that they buy out of curiosity but never really use what they buy. You gain credibility if you can identify leading-edge customers only if the customers actually *use* your product or service.

IXOS Software, Inc. (a subsidiary of the German company IXOS Software AG, in Munich) produces software that helps companies manage e-business documents. There are software packages that manage documents such as purchase orders, invoices, orders, and e-mails. Getting these documents to the right people at the right time irrespective of computer systems, and keeping them available in storage, are not trivial issues. Making the documents follow the flow of the business requires considerable skill and software flexibility. IXOS provides that skill and software.

In one area, customers told IXOS that the problem outstrips the ability of any vendor to manage the process. Large financial institutions on Wall Street have quantities of e-mail that the firms must manage in the correct manner. "Correct" becomes very specific. With millions of dollars at stake in some e-mail messages, maintaining security, errorless workflow, and regulatory compliance are critical. The quantities of e-mails are enormous. One banking customer must store, find, route, and support 400,000 e-mails a day.

Recently, IXOS considered whether to invest in producing software for "financial services exchange archiving" and perhaps create a new market. Richard Pitts, then president and CEO of the subsidiary company IXOS Software Inc., asked his team to size the work involved. "I would have to invest resources, time, and effort. And the customer would also have to make extensive effort to build a model. . . . I have an opportunity where I can literally clean up on Wall Street. It opens up other markets as well.

"My risks are opportunity costs. This has quite a bit of risk, but tremendous upside if we are successful. Just the size and scalability of the [first] four firms alone would be [25 percent of my annual revenue budget]."[9]

Pitts chose to reduce the risk by using production trials. Unlike laboratory testing by customers, these trials get the most benefit from the customer involvement strategy discussed in Chapter 8. The benefits flow to both the supplier and the customer.

Many product and concept trials are done in a laboratory-style environment. In these tests, new products and processes are tested outside the normal production process, insulating the customer's main business from the test environment. If you fly commercial airplanes, you first test new fuels and engines without using a scheduled flight. The trial does not affect the users, but neither are they involved in the process. Often, the trial is a success but the customer never deploys the products and the users do not get to gain the benefits your team created. When that happens, you do not get a good reference.

Production trials are the next level of testing. These experiments are specifically done with the users and processes that will benefit from the improvements. Production trials give you data that you would never get from laboratory style tests. Systems that work smoothly when insulated from production work differently when the real users and processes are added. Features that seemed important in the lab may be ignored in the production. More valuably, new benefits and features may come to light in a production trial. Doing a production trial makes it easier to change all aspects of the product before they are cast in concrete.

The cost to do a production trial is substantial. However, adjusting the product set at the early stages is much less expensive than making those adjustments after your product is in full production. This learning is invaluable in new market efforts. IXOS would learn an immense amount by doing production trials, and it would reduce the risk of the product considerably. If the concepts worked, the production trials would provide credibility for IXOS that could become very useful.

Using trials also reduces risk for the customer. If the IXOS team can work inside two or three of these pilot companies, the customers will benefit from having the right people on site and involved from the very beginning. If there are problems, the customer has direct access to the people who can solve those problems. Customers are not always excited about trials, but as the severity of the problem increases, the enthusiasm for a test and solution grows as well. In this case, Pitts noted that "what [these customers] want and need will require us to do an extensive pilot. The firms are excited."[10]

Reduction of risk is only a small part of the benefit that IXOS will accrue from production trials. Highly visible trials with prestigious customers are an asset when you want to create a new market. Part of creating a new market is engendering buzz around your work. As IXOS works with these giant Wall Street firms, success will be broadcast by the users and by the analyst and media community. Buzz allows others to give you the credibility that you deserve. That success will help to establish the ideas that IXOS can use to create a new market. Of course, if the work fails, that will be broadcast as well.

Production trials may delay your new market work by months or even a year. On the other hand, the credibility of a successful trial can shave years off the time it takes to make the market successful.

Do You Need Competition to Gain Credibility?

One of the ironies of creating and dominating new markets is that you do not have competition to validate your work. The presence of several credible companies in the market can add comfort to your potential customers, investors, employees, and perhaps even you. If you have no competitors, you have the option to help some enter your market. It can make your company seem more real.

On the other hand, the presence of competition is not always necessary. A large number of users, great investors, or highly influential customers can add enough credibility to overcome the lack of competitors. You always have the option to invite competitors into the market you are making. However, when you do that the cost in margin and revenue may be high and there is no turning back. Adding competition in your market should be the last option to consider.

*   *   *

When you choose to create a new market, you can increase the chances of your success by using viral marketing, by carefully choosing your customers and investors, and by deliberately slowing the process of introducing your product to run highly visible production trials. All three of these strategies use word of mouth to help you establish credibility. Credibility is important to getting traction in a new market effort, and is an asset in dominating the market.

11

What's Next?

As you read this chapter, the economy may be booming or it might be near recession. Companies may be working to grow rapidly and create and dominate new markets, or they may be dealing with tight budgets and massive disruption. These cycles continue, but they do not control whether you have an opportunity to create and dominate new markets. In either case, that opportunity is yours. You will find that changes in demographics, growth, recession, and dislocation may all increase your chances for success.

Opportunities from Changing Demographics

A normal but damaging error is to assume that yesterday's customers will be there for you tomorrow. Things change, people move, businesses age, contacts get promoted or retire, new people come in, and populations shift. In dramatic cases, populations even die out. Each change means that a market on which you count may not be stable.

You should challenge assumptions as fundamental as the makeup of the U.S. population. Today, it appears that so-called nontraditional households outnumber traditional families by three to one. The preliminary results of the 2000 census indicate that traditional families, defined as married couples with children who are 18 or younger, make up 23.5 percent of all households, approximately *half* what they were in 1960. The baby boomer generation is now in its fifties. Boomers are buying different products than they did in the 1990s. Today, there are fewer young adults between 20 and 34 years of age as a percentage of the population than the decade before.

The same changes are happening overseas. China's population is evolving quickly, and the residents have different needs today than they had yesterday. In other countries, segments of the population are disappearing. HIV is crippling the economic engine of some countries. War is destroying the economic infrastructure of others. Each of these changes means that you could be losing access to some groups of customers as you gain access to others.

Changes in consumer demographics lead to changes in corporate demographics as well. As populations increase and decrease, the businesses that serve them have no choice but to fluctuate. As those businesses adapt, a chain reaction collapses some markets and opens opportunities for you to create others. You don't sell to populations, you sell to individuals. The key is to understand where groups of individuals will be so you can involve them. In a short period of time you will discover new groups, with new needs. Changing demographics can assist your new market efforts.

For example, from the 1970s through today, the populations in North America and Europe have aged. In the United States at least, home ownership has increased at a much faster rate than new home starts. This rapid increase in home ownership created an opportunity for renovation products. In 1979 Home Depot opened its first "box store" in Atlanta. "We helped create a market of male and female 'weekend warriors' who confidently glide from project to project—and call on us for assistance whenever they hit a rough spot."[1] The company went on to create a new market for warehouse-style home repair centers, a market Home Depot still dominates. In this century, the company is expanding into South America and other locales, taking advantage of the same economic changes. A shift in population dynamics uncovered needs that became an opportunity for a new market.

Looking prospectively, as the number of single mother households increases so does the need for health insurance tailored for their needs. It may be difficult, but if an insurer is able to find a way to create a product that can provide insurance for that increasing number of homes, that company may be able to create and dominate a new market.

Opportunities from Warp-Speed Growth

When some of the economy starts to race ahead, needs increase significantly. In the 1990s, the dramatic increase in the number of dot-com companies gave rise to new markets to serve them. The personal communications market has boomed in the past decade, making for many opportunities to create new markets. The early part of this century may see impressive growth, worldwide, in residential construction. As growth occurs, new and unmet needs arise. Many of these unmet needs could spawn a new market.

One problem with rapid growth is the perception that everyone else is creating new markets and that there are none left to create. For many executives and managers, this environment seems very limited and they may feel as if they are contending with others to create the "next new thing."

This perception was rampant during the dot-com buildup,

when I would hear from owners and managers who wanted to get into the Internet world, but didn't have any idea what they should sell or do. Some of them simply copied the business plans of earlier entrants. That created a stable of online pet stores and a suite of online furniture dealers. However, it didn't create successful markets or even businesses. Many companies tested the waters and found that simply being online was not enough.[2]

The sense of competition for new markets evaporates when you remember to work from the problem instead of the product. Most of the rivalry to create the next best thing comes from companies that are product-focused. If you focus on understanding the needs of potential customers and then look for solutions, you will find that you have much less competition.

Another problem is getting attention from customers who are growing rapidly. When a company is stable, the management has the time and resources to measure and consider more opportunities. When the company is growing rapidly, all but the most critical opportunities are likely to get ignored. If you wish to succeed, choose a problem to solve that is one of the top two or three on your prospective customers' list.

You can and should assume that rapid growth periods will come and go in cycles. Each period will open gaps in potential, creating needs that customers will pay to resolve. Your problem is in anticipating the needs. In all likelihood, you won't be able to correctly guess needs. A better strategy, discussed in Chapters 7 and 8, is to get closer and closer to your potential customers and help them explore their largest problems. As you understand what keeps them from growing as fast as they wish, you will find the opportunities to create and then dominate new markets. Rapid growth can work in your favor.

Opportunities from Recession

As the overall business environment cools and seems to shrink, companies pull in their operations and slow expansion. Some cut staff, divest parts of their business, or reduce spending on nonessential parts of the company. Companies have less money to spread around, and the common lore is that markets shrink during recessions. That lore, like so many common perceptions, is not always correct.

Recessions are real in an economic sense; they are broad trends that affect groups of companies. However, in the same way that individual people are not average, neither are companies.

Very few people carry exactly the average weight for their height. Some people will be above that average, many below. If Department of Motor Vehicles records in a particular state show that the average driver is twenty-six years old, male, with brown hair and brown eyes and five foot ten inches tall, you will still find very few drivers in cars that meet that exact description. Some will have one attribute but none of the others. The more mature, shorter, blonde, blue-eyed women will make up the average, but resemble it in no way.

The same is true for business. If the average company in your business sector is slowing, some will be above that average and some below. In the spring of 2001, Lucent Technologies may have been the closest, in profit, to an average network products company. Nortel Networks was well below that, Cisco Systems above average, and Juniper Networks far above average. In a recession, your own company will be above or below average. You may not have much control over the business segment, but you have considerable control over where you are in relation to average. You can be the Nortel or the Juniper of your segment.

The equities markets may not recognize this fact. You may find your stock prices tied to the perception of the overall market. This could hamper your cash position, and a lower stock value may cause you to change your reward strategies for your teams. However, it does not reflect your ability to create and then dominate new markets.

Every time the economy slides into recession, some companies find their profits at or below the average. Lower profit levels generate pain for owners, employees, and customers. That pain reflects unmet needs, many of which are known issues. These needs may have been around during the growth periods, but were not critical.

In a recession, that might change. For instance, most companies have to write off inventory as they grow. Often, that inventory write-off is not critical as sales continue to increase. When sales decline, though, the write-offs can become a major problem. A sudden decline in sales led both Palm, Inc. and Cisco Systems to declare substantial amounts of inventory nearly worthless in the spring of 2001, at a cost of billions of dollars. These were challenges that no one was able to help them resolve. If you have a service or product that can help companies to deal with write-offs, a recession can be good for your business.

An IBM salesperson once told me that pain is good for sales. That is also true for creating and dominating new markets. Recessions offer you many more chances to find and resolve pain. Those chances can become gain for your company.

Opportunities from Dislocation, Disruption, and Consolidation

The same opportunities arise during periods of dislocation, disruption, and consolidation in markets and businesses. Even as the economy for a country or region seems stable, many businesses inside that region or country face difficult growth patterns. The business for e-mail products may grow at the expense of the sales for fax machines, though as the two curves move considerably over time (see Figure 11-1), the average stays the same. A population's move from downtown to the suburbs also

Figure 11-1. Looking past the average.

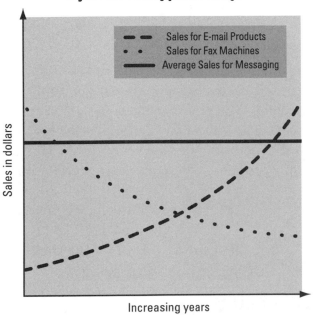

While the market for messaging products shows no substantial change, the changes in fax machines and e-mail products represent both considerable change and opportunity.

causes disruptions that can lead to new market opportunities in one segment or another.

Consolidations do the same. When banks started to consolidate in the 1980s and 1990s, the overall level of retail banking did not change. Looking at the average, you see the same numbers of accounts with the same dollars. What has changed is that retail customers concentrate their accounts into a smaller number of financial institutions. On a global level, little changed in the markets.

Looking past the averages, you can see that many banking customers found themselves without service when they needed it. Almost overnight, a new market existed: personalized banking for businesses. That new market in turn created a new set of markets for services supporting small, local banks. In the end, none may survive, but at least now we can see how a consolidation created new opportunities.

Most people are tempted to look at the averages and declare that a business segment is stable. Whenever you peel back the veneer of stability, you find that businesses are creating and satisfying needs on an almost daily basis. Each need represents a new market opportunity of which you could take advantage. Dislocation, disruption, and consolidation can work in your favor.

The Best Solution: Creating and Dominating New Markets

Whether the economic conditions trend up or down, you will have opportunities to create and dominate new markets. The broader economic trends can act either to disrupt your efforts or accelerate them.

Recessions, rapid growth, and disruption all amplify a fundamental strategy error. If you build your new market strategy on a product, these trends get in the way. The wider economic trends will sap the mind share from your prospective customers because these buyers will focus attention on their very top concerns. At the same time, under stress, consumers and managers will take less time to understand new ideas and products. They may know that they need to set time aside for new ideas, but doing so is another issue. Unless finding new ideas is as important to them as the top two problems on their list, you will find that your new product or concept gets less attention than you want. Even that can work to your benefit.

The gain comes from the tendency of almost all executives

and managers to push product instead of problems. When you discuss problems first, and truly listen to what your potential customers have to say, the advantage flows to you. Then you have taken a key step in the effort to create and then dominate a new market.

When you lead with products, these broad trends work against you. However, when you focus first on problems, the same trends give you more raw material. Disruption and stress give you better information on which problems matter the most. When you are willing to abandon a product orientation, you can choose the problem that will give you the best chance of success.

The best news is that if you lead with problems in times economic disruption, you will never have a shortage. You can always be assured of opportunity and of people and companies who will want your assistance. You may need to narrow your work to only one opportunity, and find that you can fund that effort without relying on outsiders. As you find the new worries that really disrupt your customers' lives and business, you can work with them to create new markets. When you follow the correct path, and work on ways to increase your credibility in the market, you can increase the odds of your success and satisfaction.

The future is good. You will find people to serve and markets for your business to create. You can use the information in this book to succeed. Irrespective of the economic climate, you can create and then dominate new markets when you are ready.

Notes

Chapter 1

1. Kara Swisher, *aol.com: How Steve Case Beat Bill Gates, Nailed the Netheads, and Made Millions in the War for the Web* (New York: Times Business, 1998), p. 90.

2. J. P. Donlan, "Now for the Hard Part," *Chief Executive* (September 1, 1999), p. 36, as quoted in *The Wall Street Journal* (October 18, 2000), p. 1.

3. For more on the Pointcast story, see Ken Auletta, "The Last Sure Thing," *The New Yorker* (November 9, 1998), p. 40.

Chapter 2

1. For more details on the initial years for Palm Computing, see Peter Meyer, *Warp-Speed Growth* (New York: AMACOM, 2000), chapter 10, "Resource Strategies: Growth and Technology," p. 167.

2. This story is taken from Vance Trimble, *Overnight Success: Federal Express and Frederick Smith, Its Renegade Creator* (New York: Crown Publishers, 1993), p. 112.

3. Pui-Wing Tam, "Market for Hand-Held Computers Doubled in 2000," *The Wall Street Journal* (January 25, 2001), p. B6.

4. Comments are from the author's conversation with Donald Francis, CEO of VaxGen, Inc., spring 2001, Brisban, CA (at VaxGen headquarters).

5. Frederick P. Brooks, Jr., *The Mythical Man-Month: Essays on Software Engineering*, Anniversary Edition (Boston: Addison Wesley, 1995), p. 17.

6. Jan Brandt, as quoted in Kara Swisher, *aol.com: How Steve Case Beat Bill Gates, Nailed the Netheads, and Made Millions in the War for the Web* (New York: Times Business, 1998), p.102.

7. Author's conversation with Don Francis, spring 2001.

8. For more details on the threat AIDS poses to the security of developed countries, please see the CIA report *The Global Infectious Disease Threat and Its Implications for the United States*, Document NIE 99-17D (January 2000). Available from: http://www.cia.gov/cia/publications/nie/report/nie99-17d.html (accessed September 10, 2001).

Chapter 3

1. "**create:** verb [with OBJ.] bring (something) into existence. ORIGIN late Middle English (in the sense 'form out of nothing,' used of a divine or supernatural being): from Latin *creat-*'produced,' from the verb *creare*." From the online *New Oxford Dictionary of English*, exclusively for AOL.

2. Potential has two meanings here. One is the noun that implies existing configurations of a market waiting for you to find it. The other, and more correct meaning for this purpose, is a "capacity to become or develop into something in the future." Again, see the *New Oxford Dictionary of English* (ibid.): "**potential:** adjective [ATTRIB.] having or showing the capacity to become or develop into something in the future: *a two-pronged*

campaign to woo potential customers. ORIGIN late Middle English: from late Latin *potentialis,* from *potentia* 'power,' from *potent-* 'being able' (see **POTENT**)."

3. Peter Meyer, *Warp-Speed Growth* (New York: AMACOM 2000), chapter 11, "Applications: Plan for Technology and Take Advantage of the Disruption," p. 181.

4. Ibid. chapter 3, "What Keeps the CEO Up at Night: Worries of Not Finding New Markets and Good People," p. 28.

5. This information was gathered from a survey conducted specifically for this book by the Meyer Group in 2001. Over 400 managers and executives were asked to identify the top two operational problems on their desk at the time. If you would like more information on the results, please send a request to OpsSurvey@MeyerGrp.com.

Chapter 4

1. Ralph Sarotte, General Product Manager—Minivan Platform, Daimler Chrysler Corporation. Quote supplied by Daimler Chrysler.

2. "Total Cost of Printing," *PC Magazine* (December 8, 2000). Available from: http://www.zdnet.com/pcmag/stories/reviews/0,6755,2660144,00.html (accessed September 10, 2001).

3. These numbers are from the U.S. Department of Transportation, American Express, and United Airlines.

4. The ZapMail story is told in greater detail in Vance Trimble, *Overnight Success: Federal Express and Frederick Smith, Its Renegade Creator* (New York: Crown Publishers, 1993), pp. 282–283.

Chapter 5

1. "GlaxoSmithKline to Test AIDS Vaccine on Humans," *The Wall Street Journal* (February 23, 2001).

Chapter 6

1. One such company is Contact America in Capistrano Beach, CA at (949) 443-9971.

2. David Rosenbaum, "It's Safer at the Top," *CIO Magazine* (June 15, 1999). The article quotes a survey titled "Chief Executives Say Information Technology Fails to Meet Expectations," conducted by the Compass Group.

Chapter 7

1. Wylie Wong, "Cisco Dumps Acquired Optical Technology," CNET News.com (April 4, 2001). Available from: http://news.cnet.com/news/0-1004-200-5510096.html (accessed September 10, 2001).

2. Larry Barrett, "Cisco's $2.25 Billion Mea Culpa," CNET News.com (May 9, 2001). Available from: http://news.cnet.com/news/0-1004-200-5867112.html (accessed September 10, 2001).

3. The Gauss story comes from Peter Meyer and Thijs Menzel, "Customer-Driven Markets: Recent Lessons from the Field," which originally appeared in the (Vol. 47:1, October–December 2000) issue of *Business & Economic Review*, published by the Division of Research, The Moore School of Business, The University of South Carolina (pp. 18–21). Reprinted with permission.

Chapter 8

1. The strategy described comes from conversations between the author and executives at Siemens ICN, spring 2000, Illinois.

2. Jan Carlzon, *Moments of Truth* (New York: Harper & Row, 1989).

3. For further details on the comparison of wireless network products from Lucent, Proxim, and Cisco Systems, see Peter Meyer, "Wireless Network Lessons," *Business & Economic Review* (Vol. 47:3 April 2001), pp. 28, 29.

Chapter 9

1. For a closer look at how executives at Apple Computer, Inc. wanted to change the world with computers, see John Sculley with John Byrne, *Odyssey: Pepsi to Apple* (New York: Harper & Row, 1987).

2. Ibid.

3. Comments taken from the author's conversations with Teri Fontenot, CEO of Woman's Hospital in 1999–2001 in Florida and Louisiana.

4. Comments taken from the author's conversation with Karen Brunett, director of marketing, Internet Business Solutions Group (IBSG), Cisco Systems, Inc. in spring 2000 in California.

Chapter 10

1. For a review of the history of Gnutella and its current status, look at http://www.gnutella.wego.com/.

2. Comments are from the author's private correspondence with Scott Kriens, CEO, Juniper Networks, Inc., spring 2001 in California.

3. G. Christian Hill, "Four Makers of Telecom Equipment Join to Invest in Project to Speed Up Internet," *The Wall Street Journal* (August 29, 1997), p. B10.

4. Ibid.

5. Ibid.

6. David Lazarus, "Juniper Girds for Router War with Cisco," Wired News (August 29, 1997). Available from: http:// www.wired.com/news/business/0,1367,6492,00.html (accessed September 10, 2001).

7. Author's private correspondence with Scott Kriens, spring 2001.

8. Ibid.

9. Comments based on the author's conversations with Richard Pitts, president and CEO, IXOS Software Inc., in spring 2001 in California.

10. Ibid.

Chapter 11

1. Bernie Marcus and Arthur Blank, *Built from Scratch: How a Couple of Regular Guys Grew the Home Depot from Nothing to $30 Billion* (New York: Andelman—Times Business, 1999), p. xviii.

2. For an interesting overview of one such dot-com company, Furniture.com, see "E-Commerce (A Special Report): The Lessons We've Learned," *The Wall Street Journal* (October 23, 2000). Furniture.com closed in November 2000.

Index

Adams, Ansel, 100
AIDS, 47, 104, 109, *see also* HIV
AIDSVAX, 36, 44
airline industry, 78–79, 135–136
Aironet, 177, 178
Allen, Paul, 142
alternative currencies, paying in, 138
Amazon.com, x, 145
America Online (AOL), 5, 49, 53, 173, 187
  "brainless" installation of, 177–178
  early marketing efforts by, 146–147
  and Gnutella, 204–205
  and Internet services market, 21
  and Mirabilis, 7
  as self-tailoring product, 163–164, 172
  timing of marketing by, 39–42
Andreesen, Marc, 97
anticipating problems, 72–75

AOL, *see* America Online
AOL Instant Messager, 7, 147
Apple Computer, x, xii, 10, 38, 75, 142, 162, 182–183
Apple Lisa, 182
Apple Newton, 182–183
Armstrong, C. Michael, 22–23
Ashton-Tate, 142
asking about problems, 79–89
Aspect Communications, 117, 119, 120, 132
Aspect Telecommunications, 117
AT&T Corporation, 23, 75, 101, 183
AZT, 8, 9, 104–105, 109

baby boomers, 218
Ballmer, Steve, 142
banking industry, 83–84, 223–224
Bell Laboratories, 162, 183, 184
Benchmark Capital, 211
benefits of new markets, ix–x, 4–7
Bill & Melinda Gates Foundation, 46

233

BMW, 206

Boeing Co., 208–209

Brooks, Frederick, on childbearing, 37

Brunett, Karen, 199

Burroughs Wellcome, 8, 9, 104

business leader, role of, 12–15

Cable News Network (CNN), 183, 184

California Franchise Tax Board (FTB), 136

Carlzon, Jan, 173–174, 190

Case, Steve, 21, 147

Casio, Inc., 38

CBXs, *see* Computerized Branch Exchanges

Celgene Corporation, xi, 14, 165

cellular phones, 33, 102–104, 162

Centric Software, Inc., 205–206, 212

CEOs, concerns of, 62, 193–196

Cerf, Vinton, 210

China, 218

Chrysler, 32, 73–74

Cisco Systems, Inc., 63, 177, 178, 210, 221

   inventory writeoffs by, 222

   IT function at, 191, 198–200

   and optical networking market, 143

   product development cycle at, 188

Clark, Jim, 97

CNN, *see* Cable News Network

comfortable technologies, 187

common denominators, 118–121, 128–132

Compaq Computer, 134

competition, and credibility, 215–216

competitive markets, xi

CompuServe, 40, 41, 49, 160, 177

Computer Intelligence, 130

Computerized Branch Exchanges (CBXs), 167–169

consolidations, 222–224

Continental Airlines, Inc., 206

cooking, 52, 53

core competencies, 162

costs, 17–18

   controlling, 63, 64, 68

   opportunity, 42–50

creating new markets, 51–54

creating problems, 75–79

credibility, achieving, 201–216

   by choosing the right customers/investors, 205–212

   and need for competition, 215–216

   through production trials, 212–215

   through viral marketing, 202–205

cross-functional teams, 11–12

Crosspoint Venture Partners, 211

customer-driven markets, 10

customers

   choosing, 205–209

   data on existing, 127–128

differentiating products in the eyes of prospective, 156–157
first, 207–209
getting input from, 146–147
identifying prospective, 115–118
increasing opportunities by involving, 161–176
and self-tailoring products, 163–165, 169–172
selling known products to known, 105–107
selling known products to unknown, 101–105
selling unknown products to known, 99–101
selling unknown products to unknown, 95–99
talking with, 22
working with, x

databases, *see* opportunity databases
D&B, *see* Dun & Bradstreet
dBase, 142
delivery staff, 33
Dell Computer, 134
DeLorean Motor Company, 74
demographic changes, 217–219
deodorant, 61
digital subscriber line (DSL), 176, 178
direct marketing, 39
dislocations, 222, 224
disruptions, 222–224

DOS, 23
dot-coms, 98, 186
Dow Jones & Company, 21
dreams, funding, 138–139
DSL, *see* digital subscriber line
Dubinsky, Donna, 32
Dun & Bradstreet (D&B), 120–121, 127, 130, 131
DUNS number, 127–128, 130

economic growth, 219–220
EDI (electronic data interchange), 92
Edsel (automobile), 74
effects, billing users for, 135–136
electric cars, 98
electronic data interchange (EDI), 92
employees, recruiting, x
enterprise resource planning (ERP), 175
Epogen, 50
Ericsson, 103, 212
ERP (enterprise resource planning), 175
Estridge, Don, 142
excitement of new markets, 4
extranets, 148
eyeballs, 25

failure, risk of, 107–109
fax machines, 13–14, 146, 203
FDA, *see* Food and Drug Administration
Federal Express, 32–33, 52, 90–91, 99

Federal Reserve, 99
finance team, 15
first to market acceptance, 155
floor coatings, 57–58
Fontenot, Teri, 197, 198
Food and Drug Administration
    (FDA), xi, 36, 164
Forbes, Malcom, Jr., on time, 38
Ford, Henry, 10
Ford Motor Company, 74
Francis, Dr. Donald, 37, 42–49,
    107
FTB (Franchise Tax Board), 136
functional issues, day-to-day,
    65–66
funding issues, 17–18

Gates, Bill, 21, 142
Gauss (technology company), 83,
    84, 148–153
Genentech, 43, 47, 50
General Dynamics Corporation,
    208
General Electric, 21, 183
General Motors, 206
GlaxoSmithKline, 8, 49
Glaxo Wellcome, 10–11
Gnutella, 204–205
"great ideas," 19–20
growth, rapid, 219–220
GTE Defense, 208

HandEra, 165, 189
handheld computers, 34–35, 183
Handspring, 165, 189

Harte-Hanks Market Intelligence,
    130, 131
Hawkins, Jeff, 32
Hewlett-Packard, 77, 78, 134
HIV (human immunodeficiency
    virus), xi, 8, 9, 27–28, 31, 36–
    37, 43–47, 49, 50, 104, 105,
    164, 218
Home Depot, 218–219
hot technologies, 186
hurdles to success, 17–22

IBM Corporation, 19, 21, 23, 109,
    134, 142, 165, 167
IBM OS2, 173
Imitrex, 11
independence, x
informational interviews, 81–89
    callbacks following, 88–89
    conducting, 87–88
    identifying targets for, 83–85
    and problem solving, 89
    setting up, 85
    structuring questions for, 86–87
information-related problems, 66
information technology (IT) func-
    tion, 66, 132–139, 181,
    191–200
    alternative currencies used by,
    138
    and billing users for effects,
    135–136
    and CEO concerns, 193–196
    at Cisco Systems, 191, 198–200
    funding the dreams of, 138–139

renting by, 133–134
as tool for new markets, 196–198
traditional focus of, 192
as venture capitalist, 136–138
infrastructure problems, 66
inkjet printers, 75–78
instant messaging, 7, 147
instant photography, 52–53, 164
Institutional Venture Partners, 211
Integrated Services Digital Network (ISDN), 10, 24, 56, 74–75
Internet economy, 26
Internet service providers (ISPs), 5
Internet services, 21
intranets, 148
investors, choosing, 209–212
ISDN, *see* Integrated Services Digital Network
ISPs (Internet service providers), 5
IT function, *see* information technology function
ITT Automotive, 206
IXOS Software, Inc., 212–215

Jobs, Steve, xi, xii, 10, 141–142, 182
Juniper Networks, Inc., 206, 209–212, 221

Kleiner, Perkins, Caulfield & Byers, 211
KLM Royal Dutch Airlines, 206
KPMG Consulting, Inc., 138
Kriens, Scott, 209–212
Kyocera, 165

Land, Edwin, 8, 11, 53, 99, 100
leadership, 11–12
Leeds Company, 150–152, 156
LEGO, 164, 172, 173
Lexmark, 78
line extensions, market creators vs., 8–9
Lockheed Martin, 19, 109, 184, 208, 209
LOMAC, 142
Los Alamos Scientific Laboratories, 208
Lucent Technologies, 177, 178, 212, 221

Macintosh computer, 142, 182
manufacturing staff, 33
mapping, sales opportunity, 121–124
Mardix, 207–209
market creators, line extensions vs., 8–9
marketing
with opportunity databases, 116
viral, 202–205
marketing staff, 33
marketing team, 13–14
market(s)
customer-driven vs. vendor-driven, 10–11
finding vs. creating, 52
new, *see* new markets
predicting, 145
shaping, 144

Maslow, Abraham, on men with
    hammers, 34
McDonnell Douglas, 208, 209
McKenna, Regis, 23, 154–155, 205
m-commerce, 145
meeting technology, 120
Merck, 49
Meyer Group, The, 62, 63, 193
Microsoft Corporation, 5, 21, 23–
    24, 34, 72, 97, 138, 142, 189
Microsoft Network (MSN), 5
Microsoft Windows operating
    system, 23, 34, 173
migraine, 11
minivans, 73–74
Mirabilis Ltd., 7
mistakes, making, ix, 6
Mitsubishi Electric, 19
"moments of truth," 173–174
money
    as problem, 61–62
    as resource, 29–33
Mosaic Communications, 96–97
Mossberg, Walter, on technology,
    175
Motorola, Inc., 11, 103–104, 162,
    165
MSN (Microsoft Network), 5
Music Television (MTV), 183

Napster Inc., 202–203
needs, 27–28
Netscape Communications, 10,
    11, 96–98, 138
Neupogen, 50

Newbridge Networks, 212
new economy, 26
New Enterprise Associates, 211
new markets
    benefits of, ix–x, 4–7
    characteristics of, 7–9
    within companies, 198–200
    creating, 51–54
    excitement of, 4
    finding vs. creating, 27
    forgiving nature of, 5–7
    hurdles to success in, 17–22
    location of, 9
    paths to, 12, 13
    pitfalls when building, 159–161
    potential for, 27–28
    profitability of, 4–5
    questions to ask to build, 16–17
    success factors in, 10–12
niches, identifying, 118
Nike, x
Nokia Corporation, 103
noncustomers, looking at, 127
nontraditional households, 218
Nortel Networks, 103, 212, 221
Northrop Corporation, 208
Nowinski, Robert, 42, 43
NPD Intelect, 34–35

OmniSky Corporation, 206, 208
operational management, top
    problems of, 62–68
opportunities, purposely ignor-
    ing, 11
opportunity costs, 42–50

opportunity databases, 114–132
  and identification of prospec-
    tive customers, 115–118
  identifying common denomi-
    nators in, 118–121
  mapping territory based on,
    121–124
  noncustomers as second, 127
  steps for creating, 127–132
  team for building, 124–127
  traditional lead programs vs.,
    115
optical networking, 143
Orinoco, 177, 178
Osborne Computer, 142, 145, 160

Pacific Bell, 75–76
pain, selling, 57–59
Palm, Inc., 32, 34–35, 38, 61, 165,
    173, 183, 189–190, 206–207,
    222
PDAs, *see* personal digital assis-
    tants
people
  as concern of CEOs, 195–196
  as resource, 29–30, 33–35
PepsiCo, xii
perceived needs, 28
personal digital assistants (PDAs),
    32, 34–35, 38, 189, 206
pharmaceutical industry, xi, 8, 9,
    10–11, 14, 31, 42–50, 104–105,
    107, 109
Philadelphia, 137
Picturephone, 101

Pitts, Richard, 213
Pointcast, 7, 25–26
Polaroid Corporation, 8, 52–53,
    100, 183
Post-it Notes, 98
potential, 51–57
predicting the market, 145
prioritizing, 60, 131–132
problem(s)
  anticipating, 72–75
  asking about, 79–89
  of CEOs, 62
  changing severity of, 92
  creating, 75–79
  failure from success in solving,
    91
  identifying, 20, 60–61
  money as, 61–62
  of operational management,
    62–68
  pain caused by, 58–59
  as potential, 54–57
  willingness to abandon wrong,
    89–91
Prodigy, 40, 41, 49, 177
Productivity Bank, 137
products
  building customer involvement
    into, 165–169
  consumer-definable, 163–165,
    169–172
profitability, x, 4–5
Proxim, 177, 178
Psion PLC, 38
push technology, 24–26

quadraphonic sound, 55–56

razor blades, 75
recession, opportunities from, 220–222
renting, 133–134
resource(s), 29–42
  money as, 30–33
  people as, 33–35
  time as, 35–42
return on investment (ROI), 62
risk(s), 11
  of failure, 107–109
  taking, 15–16
ROI (return on investment), 62
ROLM, 165–169
Russo, Carl, on optical networking, 143

Saab, 206
sales channels, 116
sales team, 14–15
sales training, 58–59
Sandia National Laboratories, 208
Sarotte, Ralph, on minivans, 73
SAS (airline), 173
Sculley, John, xii, 182
Sears, 21
self-tailoring, 163–165, 169–172
serendipity, 14
shaping the market, 144
SIC codes, 129
Siemens, 212
Siemens ICN, 165–168
skill requirements, 19

Skunkworks, 19, 184
Smith, Frederick, 32, 33, 99
Sony Corporation, 162, 165, 183, 184, 187, 189
Sprint, 165
Spyglass, Inc., 97
stock value, x, 5
support, finding, 18
Swissair, 206
Symphony (Proxim), 177, 178

Tang, 20
team(s)
  for building opportunity databases, 124–127
  cross-functional, 11–12
  finance, 15
  marketing, 13–14
  sales, 14–15
technology(-ies)
  choosing among, 184–188
  "comfortable," 187
  computer, 185
  and creation of new markets, 182–183
  customer difficulties with, 175
  effect vs., 172–173
  "hot," 186
  for meetings, 120
  and needs gap, 188–191
  repeatedly making new markets with, 183–184
  see also information technology function
technology upgrade programs, 134

Thalomid (thalidomide), xi, 14, 164–165
3Com, 32, 212
3M, 98
Tide brand detergent, 8–9, 105, 106
time, ix, 22–24
and predicting the market, 145–146
as resource, 30, 35–42
as website issue, 152
time to market acceptance, 23
TiVo, 170–171
trends, 186

United Airlines, 206
Upside magazine, 98
U.S. Robotics, 32
UUNET, 212

VaxGen, Inc., 36–37, 42–50, 107
vendor-driven markets, 10
venture capitalist, IT as a, 136–138
viral marketing, 202–205
VisiCalc, 142
visionaries, x, 10
voice-mail systems, 135
Volvo, 206
VSIS, Inc., 19

The Wall Street Journal, 210
Wal-Mart Stores, Inc., 142, 185
Walton, Sam, 142
WAP (Wireless Application Protocol), 145
websites, 148–154
Webvan, 7, 55, 74
Windows operating system, *see* Microsoft Windows operating system
Wireless Application Protocol (WAP), 145
Woman's Hospital (Baton Rouge, LA), 197–198, 200
word of mouth, 203–204
WordPerfect, 23
word processors, 23–24
World Bank, 45
WorldCom Inc., 212
World Wide Web (WWW), 96–98
Wozniak, Steve, 10
WWW, *see* World Wide Web

Xerox Corporation, 162

Yahoo!, 5

ZapMail, 90–91
ZD Market Intelligence, 130
zip codes, mapping opportunities by, 121